When God Winks

When God Winks

How the Power of Coincidence Guides Your Life

NOW WITH A NEW AUTHOR'S NOTE

SQuire Rushnell

HOWARD BOOKS

New York   London   Toronto   Sydney   New Delhi

HOWARD BOOKS

An Imprint of Simon & Schuster, Inc.
1230 Avenue of the Americas
New York, NY 10020

First Howard Books trade paperback edition September 2018

HOWARD and colophon are trademarks of Simon & Schuster, Inc.

For information about special discounts for bulk purchases, please contact Simon &
Schuster Special Sales at 1-866-506-1949 or business@simonandschuster.com.

The Simon & Schuster Speakers Bureau can bring authors to your live event. For more
information or to book an event, contact the Simon & Schuster Speakers Bureau at
1-866-248-3049 or visit our website at www.simonspeakers.com.

Manufactured in the United States of America

10 9 8 7 6 5 4

Library of Congress Cataloging-in-Publication Data

ISBN 978-0-7434-6707-0
ISBN 978-1-9821-0726-0 (pbk)
ISBN 978-0-7434-7086-5 (ebook)

Dear Reader:

This book will validate your feelings that there's more to so-called "coincidence" than meets the eye.

It also fosters hope for the dreams of your future by unveiling the wondrous map that has quietly guided you along the paths of your past.

God has been winking at you.

SQuire Rushnell

P.S. Please contact me when these promises come true. Write to stories@godwinks.com or visit www.godwinks.com

P.P.S. Yes, in case you are wondering, the "Q" in my name is supposed to be capitalized.

CO·IN·CI·DENCE

A sequence of events that although accidental seems to have been planned or arranged.

WINK

To give a signal or express a message.

—*American Heritage Dictionary*

GODWINK

1. Not a coincidence but an event or experience so astonishing it must be of divine origin.
2. Another term for answered prayer.

—*The author*

Contents

Contents

Acknowledgments

I am deeply grateful for the support of my darling wife, Louise—my spiritual guide—and my daughter Robin for her skillful editorial assistance, and Marian Christy, a wonderful writer whose wisdom this book reflects. I also thank each of you—and you know who you are—who, along the way, helped God nudge me in the right direction.

Author's Note

An Update of the Original Godwinks Book

It may have been a Godwink itself that this book about hope and encouragement arrived on bookshelves in late summer 2001. America was about to be shaken to the core. Our nation was soon to be attacked by foreign forces with no motive other than incomprehensible hate and the desire to rob us of our joy. We stared in shock as the World Trade Centers in New York tumbled into ashes and our country's military headquarters became engulfed in flames.

For a brief moment the television images sapped our hope.

Then, America came together—the *United* States of America. We dug deeply into our inner spirits and found comfort in God's promises and began to see things from a wider perspective, and even learned to acknowledge mysterious, supernatural experiences—things that we were maybe too busy to notice earlier—messages of reassurance that were being sent directly to each of us, to lift our spirits, and provide a tangible handrail to a benevolent force who was up there watching over us.

As we struggled to find a name for these wondrous events, the word "coincidence" seemed odd and inadequate. If we understood the Hebrew language, we'd have known that the word didn't even exist.

As the final act before this book was delivered to the publisher, my dear wife, Louise, and I initiated a quest— what do you call a coincidence that isn't a coincidence?

For several months we wrestled endlessly with that question, prayed about it, and then, one day, the little word "Godwink" simply floated into my mind. *That's a fun, non-threatening word*, I thought. I went back to the manuscript and began replacing the term "coincidence" with "Godwink."

It fit! More important, readers instantly began using the word to fill the vacancy in the language.

From that moment on, you—our readers—have played an integral role in the evolution of the Godwinks Thesis. For example, readers led us to comprehend that the word "Godwink" actually has two dictionary meanings. The first describes "a mysterious event that's not coincidence, but of divine origin." The second is "another term for answered prayer." Moreover, together with our readers, we came to understand that prayer and Godwinks are inextricably connected.

In short, Godwinks are signs of hope; God's way of providing you with encouragement, comfort, and certainty. True stories prove that, in this and each of the books in the Godwinks series. I promise.

—*SQuire Rushnell*

Introduction

When I pray, coincidences happen, and when I don't, they don't.
Sir William Temple

Have you ever found yourself thinking about someone who hasn't crossed your mind in years, and then you run into that person the next day?

Or has something unpleasant happened to you—like getting laid off from your job—only to find out that you had a better opportunity a short while later?

Just before brushing off these seemingly random acts, did you find yourself quietly saying, "I-e-e-e wonder. Was that coincidence—or something more?"

As a matter of fact, what motivated you to pick up this book?

Was it chance?

Or were you led to this moment to learn more about yourself and the mysterious guideposts—what I call God-winks—that cause you to meet certain people, propel you in new directions, and place you into situations you never anticipated?

You're about to confirm something you have suspected all along: that what you thought were coincidences, were actually Godwinks, little messages to encourage you on your journey through life, nudging you along the grand path that has been designed especially for you.

This book is a simple bridge to your self-discovery.

- In part one, you'll learn ways to open your eyes to see the amazing ways that God has been working in your life.
- Then, in part two, you'll read about ways you can use Godwinks to enrich your life as you go forward. You will even learn how to create more Godwinks—turning your wishes into winks. And you'll read about everyday people, as well as celebrities, who have taken comfort in Godwinks and have found them to be empowering.
- Part three is packed with fascinating stories demonstrating that winks from God guide us through every aspect of life, from relationships to careers, from films to sporting events.

As you embark on this marvelous process of discovering the Godwinks in your life, I ask you to keep your mind open to possibilities you have never imagined and to be prepared to take action steps toward goals and dreams that may now seem distant.

Now, start turning pages, and get ready for a wonderful journey!

Unearthing the winks from your past

Almost everyone harbors a slight, rarely articulated suspicion that there might be something more to "coincidence" than meets the eye—something special and, almost always, spiritual. For this book, I have interviewed scores of people and researched hundreds of Godwink stories in hopes that a new perspective on such astonishing events would help others to enrich their own lives.

One frequent speculation was that Godwinks rarely stand alone. Many people suggested that they happen in clusters, or as a continuing series of unusual events.

Over the course of this book, I will be challenging you to take a sort of archaeological expedition into yourself. When you do, you'll be surprised to discover the emergence of an enchanting pattern of Godwinks marking your relationships and pursuits, and your ups and downs.

As you chart your winks, you'll see that they have increased in frequency at major turning points in your life: when you lost someone you love or found someone *to* love; when you reached a crossroads in your career, such as a job loss or a promotion; or when something happened that sent your life in a whole new direction.

Learning to identify Godwinks—hopeful communications directly to you out of seven billion people on the planet—will help you to develop a confident sense of direction. It will be an affirmation that, no matter how often you may think it, you are never alone. Somewhere up above, there is a universal guidance system, and you are on that radar screen.

My own revelation of Godwinks

The concept that Godwinks can be revisited to create a chronicle of past winks from God first occurred to me as I sorted through the turning points in my own life.

I focused on the moment when I first realized what I wanted to be when I grew up. It was in sixth grade. A visit to a radio station had hooked me. I wanted to be a radio announcer.

By tenth grade, I had spent four years talking into a broom handle, driving my older brother crazy, reading the newspaper aloud, forcing my voice down low like David Brinkley.

But my real hero was a morning personality on a radio station sixty miles south of my little town of Adams Center, New York. Dean Harris was an energetic disc jockey, fond of ordering his legions of listeners to get up and "march around the breakfast table" to whatever melody he was playing. And into my broom, around our breakfast table at home, I frequently emulated him, causing my brother to send a Wheaties box sailing in my direction.

- What is your first memory of what you wanted to be when you grew up?
- Can you recall how old you were? Where you were? Who was with you?
- Was there some *event*, some *place*, or some *person* that ignited your career or life interest?
- How did you go about making that first step related to your eventual career or life interest?
- Finally, can you recall a Godwink—any unusual experience or happenstance—relating to your career or life interest?

The last question is the hardest to answer. Don't worry—you're not alone. Godwinks are dismissed, repressed, and overlooked by everyone. As such, they are not easily uncovered. You need patience. And persistence. But before long, digging up Godwinks of the past will become easier, and you'll think you're mining gold out of your very own life. Before you know it, you will have learned to recognize the significance of Godwinks as they happen rather than years later.

You may have interpreted what you thought was a "coincidence" relating to your career as some silly little occurrence that happened to you once—nothing more significant. That's what happened to me; I had always recalled being picked up by my hero while hitchhiking to my first job, but it never dawned on me—until I began writing this book—that it was *actually* a remarkable sign of encouragement that I was on the right path.

Later on, I will show you that your dreams, wishes, and prayers can actually help you *cultivate* Godwinks and use them to enrich your life. By focusing on a desired outcome, you can cause Godwinks to appear all along your path.

A diary of winks

I keep a thin, narrow diary that slips nicely into an inside coat pocket or a briefcase. It's my diary of winks. Whenever a Godwink occurs, I jot it down. Or whenever there's a turning-point event that I assume will *trigger* a Godwink, I also write it down, leaving space to register the wink when it happens. More often than not, the Godwinks I record in my diary are small, everyday experiences. But while most are not earth-shattering, it has been quite eye-opening to flip back through the pages. After only a few weeks of keeping my diary, I was startled by the prolific nature of Godwinks that I used to shrug away. And I am impressed with the reaffirmation that Godwinks from above occur at every crossroads.

Try it.

Make an easy-to-use diary—perhaps a small notebook like mine, the notes app on your phone, or even a piece of paper stuck to the refrigerator door.

The important thing is to keep the diary in *sight* and not out of mind. The fleeting nature of Godwinks is that they slip into and out of our lives in a blink—so you need to get into the habit of jotting them down immediately.

My promise to you

First, you are under the influence of a built-in GPS—God's Positioning System—and every day you receive little nudges to keep you on your chosen path.

Second, tracking the Godwinks in your past will create an astonishingly lucid account of your life, while providing clarity to the grand possibilities on the road ahead.

Third, you can learn to harness the power of Godwinks to enrich your future and to strengthen your inner convictions that the life path you've chosen is indeed God's path for you.

Lastly, you'll see that Godwinks happen for a reason, and that's to let you know one thing: You are not alone.

> *In all your ways acknowledge him,*
> *and he shall direct your paths.*
>
> —PROVERBS 3:6 KJV

Part One

Opening Your Eyes to See the Winks

I

Godwinks Happen All the Time

I shall never believe that God
plays dice with the world.
Albert Einstein

Once you undertake an archaeological dig into your career you'll discover that Godwinks happen more than you thought.

Unveiling the Godwinks that occurred at times of crisis and in moments of radical change may require some diligence. The events themselves may have been so overpowering that any rational thought at all, at the time, would have seemed impossible. Yet as you undertake a revisiting of your life's crossroads, you'll be surprised and heartened to see the Godwinks that have been with you at every step of the way, providing you with signs of hope.

Finding the reassurance in the wink

Think back to when you were a child, sitting at the dinner table with the grownups. You looked up and saw a parent or grandparent smiling at you. And then they winked. That wink was a message of loving reassurance saying, "Hey, kid, I'm thinking about you. You're OK. Hang in there."

A Godwink is *also* a message of reassurance coming when you most need it: when you're at a fragile moment in your life, and when instability is all around. It might be said, in fact, that Godwinks are the best way for God to make Himself known in your life and to provide encouragement.

Think about it. If you were God and wanted to communicate with human beings without using a human voice, how would you do it?

You'd perform little miracles, wouldn't you? You'd create uplifting experiences that cause people to say, "What are the odds of this ever happening?" Those are Godwinks.

The events in the story that follows gave me great comfort during a time of high anxiety in my career. I had progressed from that long-ago day when I was hitchhiking to my first job interview, through various positions in television to an executive position at the ABC Television Network.

Had I not already been tuning in to the Godwinks from above, I might not have noticed the signs of reassurance that came my way. I might have gotten stressed out and downhearted.

When your employer is merged or taken over by another company, you have reason to worry.

It's change, and change means uncertainty.

Uncertainty means discomfort.

Many questions run through your mind: Am I going to keep my job? Even if I'm still employed, will they upset the applecart with all kinds of ideas on how to run my department? Will they be demanding meetings and reports that will drastically increase my already-heavy workload?

In early January 1986, those questions were racing through my mind as ABC was being taken over by Capital Cities Broadcasting. And while I may have looked calm on the surface, the uncertainty of the new situation continued to gnaw at me until a startling Godwink turned *uncertainty* into a feeling of *certainty*.

It began with a Friday-afternoon meeting.

All the top ABC executives on the East Coast were gathered into a large studio in New York to be introduced to our new bosses and to learn the details of the takeover.

The mission of Tom Murphy, the new CEO—long the head of Capital Cities Broadcasting—was to put everybody at ease, to advise how the transition was to take place, and to answer a few questions.

ABC anchorman Peter Jennings shot up his hand, challenging Tom Murphy with what I thought was a rather pointed question. He wanted to know if, under Capital Cities, ABC News would retain its news integrity.

Holding his cool in the face of this aggressive inquiry,

Murphy's deft reply—that television is a public trust and that it was the news operation of ABC that fostered the public's trust in it—really impressed me.

As I left for the weekend with my family to our new country home in Connecticut, Murphy's comments helped me feel a bit more secure—slightly assured that this turning point in my life—after fifteen years with ABC—was maybe going to turn out all right.

My daughter Hilary was visiting that weekend from college, and on Sunday morning she offered a soothing antidote for the tumult churning my nerve endings. She suggested we go to church.

Great idea, said I.

Then, as I was about to confess that we had not yet developed a church affiliation in the area, an image came to mind of the little church we had passed on the way over the mountain to the Grand Union in Pawling, New York.

"It sits up there like a quaint, black-shuttered, white-steepled New England church in a Grandma Moses painting," I told her. "Why don't we go there?"

It turned out to be a delightful experience and inaugurated a long commitment to a place of worship. During coffee hour on that first Sunday, several members of the congregation told how Lowell Thomas, the famed news broadcaster, had belonged to the church. They pointed to his burial place next to a big rock right behind the church.

That in itself was a Godwink which I failed to recognize until later. The esteemed Lowell Thomas was the founder of Capital Cities Broadcasting, my new employer.

The next day on a trip to my West Coast office, I carried warm thoughts about my visit to the little church on Quaker Hill. Upon arrival, I was surprised to learn that the new Capital Cities management team was also in Los Angeles. They were there that very day in order to replay, for ABC's West Coast contingent, the same transition remarks and new-management introduction that had been presented the previous Friday to the East Coast staff.

It was a smaller gathering, followed by a cocktail party that afforded me the first opportunity to meet Tom Murphy face-to-face—the man whom *Time* magazine was heralding, that very week, as "the most powerful man in broadcasting."

Boldly attempting to score points with the new boss, I told him how impressed I was with his handling of Peter Jennings's question.

A dark look instantly descended over his face.

I shuddered, realizing that I had just struck a sensitive chord.

"I've been thinking about that question all weekend," he exclaimed in an irritated manner. "I should have told Peter Jennings that with all our newspaper holdings, Cap Cities probably has more reporters than ABC. Therefore, why in the dickens would we want to change our news integrity!"

"You're absolutely right!" I chirped—his newest, most loyal sycophant. Then another thought entered my mind—something that would *really* impress the new boss. "And you could have told him that Cap Cities was founded by that great broadcast journalist Lowell Thomas," I said proudly.

"I wish I'd thought of that!" he snapped approvingly.

Now I was on a roll.

As the image of the big rock by Lowell Thomas's grave popped into my mind, I unhesitatingly decided to tell Tom Murphy something he probably didn't know. "That reminds me, Tom," I began. "This weekend my daughter and I went to a little church back East for the first time. And you know what? Lowell Thomas is buried right there behind the church!"

The way he cocked his head and narrowed his eyes made me realize that Tom Murphy was about to tell *me* something that I didn't know. "SQuire, let me tell you what the little church on Quaker Hill means to me."

(*Gulp*.)

"You know how you go out the front door of that church and look across the road at a big white house with black shutters?"

I nodded, my eyes dilating, as that image came to mind.

"Well, that was Lowell Thomas's house that I was brought to. That house is where I was offered my first job at Cap Cities."

(*Holy cannoli!*)

Hours later I was still shaking my head, incredibly astonished by what had happened over the course of a weekend and—geographically—across the country.

The mathematical odds were high that I would

- Hear Tom Murphy speak for the first time in New York City on Friday.
- Attend a little church for the first time in upstate New York on Sunday.
- Engage this man in conversation for the first time in Los Angeles on Monday to find that the common thread between us would be the small patch of land called Quaker Hill, where "the most powerful man in broadcasting" got his start.

At that anxious turning point in my life, I concluded that it had to be a sign.

A neon sign.

That little Godwink gave me confidence that I was on the right path. And aren't we all looking for that little bit of reassurance in our lives? All we have to do is recognize that Godwinks happen to us every day.

Finding your turning-point Godwinks

The following questions may help you dislodge memories and help you create an inventory of events that placed you at various crossroads in your life.

After you read each bulleted item, write down the first thoughts that come to your head. Take the time, before you start to write, to examine your life. Reflect on each question, and then let your thoughts flow. Don't be a critic; don't worry about punctuation, grammar, or even if what you write makes any sense. Just let your memory, not your rational mind, do the writing. You'll be surprised what will emerge.

- Did something surprising happen to you sometime in your past? Did you gain something unexpectedly— through an inheritance or other unplanned windfall? Did good fortune seem to come at exactly the moment you were facing overwhelming financial problems? Jot down the unexpected bonus and describe the point in your life you were at when you received it.
- Did some new person come into your life? That can be a turning point. The birth of a baby, perhaps? Did a best friend radically change the way you

looked at life—perhaps helping your faith? As you identify the life-altering event or revelation, try to recall a Godwink that seemed to confirm your new direction.

- How about personal relationships? When did you fall in love? How did you meet your love? Was there a Godwink leading up to the meeting or in the meeting itself? What about when a relationship ended—a divorce, perhaps? Any winks, in hindsight, that could have been interpreted as a sign of comfort?

- Did you experience the death of someone close to you: a parent, grandparent, or favorite aunt? Did the loss start you out on a whole new path? Or did the death of a loved one require you to move? In any case, can you remember a Godwink that accompanied that event? Was it a source of unexpected comfort?

- When did you get the biggest break in your job? It must have changed the path you were on. Was there a Godwink there as well?

- Did you have a rebirth—spiritual or otherwise? Perhaps a determination to quit what you were doing to pursue your dream? Or a firm commitment to abandon an unhealthy habit like drinking or smoking? What were the Godwinks before, during, or after your rebirth or commitment?

Don't worry if you can't answer every question. Like any skill, your ability to identify Godwinks will only get stronger with practice. And that's why you're reading this book!

Just remember to use your diary. Once you've gotten into the habit of recording the Godwinks that happen to you today, you'll be surprised how many you start to remember from your past.

As the route of your life path and your winks from God begin to emerge—like a rainbow out of the mist of your mind—you will be struck by the message of hope that it holds for you.

> *Stand at the crossroads and look . . .*
> *Ask which way leads to blessings.*
> *Live that way and find a resting place for yourselves.*
> —JEREMIAH 6:16 GW

2

You Are Part of a Universe That Is Ordered and Designed

*May not such events raise the suggestion
that they are not undesigned?*
Daniel Webster

Your life is not a series of random experiences taking you like a twig in a moving stream to destinations unknown.

You are part of a much greater plan.

Raising your consciousness to the Godwinks that often go by unnoticed or get dismissed and recognizing them as tremendously personal will reaffirm that your existence is not random and that you *do* have a role to play in God's grand plan.

A soul mate found

Sometimes life seems to get the better of us, and we lose hope that there's anything orderly about our lives. Our best attempts have failed. We're beset by problems and it seems like things will never look up again. That's what Alice Marina thought. Until she got the biggest Godwink of her life.

Alice had just about given up. "God, if you want me to be single for the rest of my life, that's OK, just put peace in my heart." Her plea exposed the pain of her depressed feelings. Every one of Alice's relationships had ended in heartbreak. Now, well into her thirties, she had come to the inescapable conclusion that there was no Cinderella story in the crystal ball of her future, and there was no Prince Charming who was going to ride into her life on a white horse.

On top of all that, she had been diagnosed with multiple sclerosis.

Covering up feelings of stress and sadness, she threw herself into the pursuit of a master's degree, pushing herself to study long and hard.

Here's where Alice started to acknowledge, consciously or not, that there is an order to the universe. She stopped struggling, and when she did that, she opened herself to seeing the unexpected and the unplanned—the Godwinks.

"If you want me to be married, God, *you* pick him out. My track record stinks."

After this surrender, the first thing that happened was a softening in her heart at her sister's repeated urging to go to a church singles group. She finally agreed to at least give it a try. Yet after a couple of hours of standing around and feeling out of place, those old familiar feelings of despair began to rise within her. She started to leave. Stepping past a man seated near the exit, her eyes were drawn to his.

"His golden-brown eyes were riveting," she said later, "and his handshake was absolutely electric." His name was Jack Totah.

They began talking. The conversation cascaded from one topic to the next for nearly three hours.

"Oh my gosh, I've got to go," exclaimed Alice. "I've got to study for an exam. I've also got to run a bunch of errands because I'm taking a trip to Texas next weekend. My cousin is getting married in Victoria."

"No kidding," said Jack, "*I'm* going to Victoria, Texas, next weekend. And *my* cousin is getting married. To a doctor."

"Really? My cousin *is* a doctor," replied an astonished Alice.

It was true. Alice Marina's cousin was marrying Jack Totah's cousin, and amazingly, these two people were both planning to go to the wedding, in a small city, seven hours away.

What a powerful wink signaling that they were on the right path!

Of course, to save on gas, Alice and Jack arranged to drive to Victoria together, and for the entire seven-hour trip they were never at a loss for words.

It was a fabulous wedding. Alice and Jack danced and

danced like they were floating on clouds. It was magical. And when Jack walked Alice to her door, he kissed her goodnight. "That kiss," gasped Alice, "made my toes curl. Wow!"

The next morning Alice was up early to meet her dear Uncle Charlie for breakfast. While telling him what a glorious time she had at the wedding, she also revealed a secret: She had met the man she was going to marry.

"He's a wonderful, wonderful man, and we enjoy so many of the same things," she whispered excitedly, "I want you to meet him. His name is Jack Totah."

"Jack Totah?" repeated Uncle Charlie. "I wonder if he's related to Nabe Totah?"

"Yes," said Jack, walking into the kitchen. "He's my uncle."

Uncle Charlie then explained to Alice and Jack that fifty years earlier he had met Nabe Totah on a boat coming to America. Both were lonely. They became fast friends, but then, when they went through customs they were separated, and lost touch completely.

That Godwink was another sign of hope for Alice.

The initial Godwink that Alice and Jack were both heading to a weekened wedding in Victoria, Texas, coupled with the incredible Godwink that their favorite uncles had a friendship that began years before confirmed the prayer that Alice had plaintively placed before God. "If you want me to be married, God, you pick him out."

Those Godwinks of encouragement helped her then to do the thing she had feared—to tell Jack about her medical condition.

"Maybe you shouldn't mention it," said a friend.

"No, I have to," she said.

Jack's response to Alice's confession that she had MS was all she could have hoped for. He looked down for a moment and then replied, "I am so sorry. Just tell me what I need to do."

A year and a half later, Alice and Jack were married. There in the front row of the wedding were their two uncles, Charlie, from West Texas, and Nabe, from Fremont, California, reawakening a friendship that had lain dormant for fifty years.

"I found my true soul mate," says Alice, "And our two uncles found each other. Thank God. I mean *really*—thank God!"

Alice is now a firm believer that there is a guiding power and an order to our lives; it may not guide us on the paths we choose for ourselves or at the pace we want it to, but it guides us nevertheless. When we carry ourselves as far as we can and feel we can go no further, that's when we should be on the lookout for a Godwink. It's coming.

If you still struggle with the idea of a world that is ordered and designed, the story that follows might help you conclude that there *is* a grand plan and that in the end, all of the pieces of the plan ultimately sort themselves in a beautiful way.

Best friends or . . .

Ron Barren and Roger Mansfield grew up within twenty miles of each other in Michigan. They had never met. They had both moved from Michigan to opposite sides of the country at about the same time: Ron to Florida, Roger to the state of Washington.

Coincidentally, they returned to Michigan at about the same time, where they both applied for a job they had seen in an ad. The Greenery Nursing Home promised training in return for an applicant's commitment to be a nursing assistant.

Both Ron and Roger applied the same day. Both were accepted and sent to a three-week class at a community college. For on-the-job training, they were assigned to the graveyard shift at the nursing home.

Ron and Roger were becoming good friends. They had the same sense of humor and constantly enjoyed joking around. One day the instructor spoke about the importance of early childhood nurturing in the development of an individual. Speaking up, Roger agreed, telling the class that as a child he had been abandoned and neglected.

Ron said the same thing had happened to him.

Soon, the two were monopolizing the class with their similar experiences. Then, in the coup de grâce, Roger mentioned that while his present name was Mansfield, his biological last name was Fletcher.

"Me too!" said Ron, flabbergasted.

Ron Barren and Roger Mansfield were brothers, two of eight siblings put up for adoption. What is remarkable is that Ron and Roger were not out looking for their long-lost sibling. They had no idea that they even *had* a brother.

Yet a string of Godwinks from above had kept them unmistakably on the same path toward each other and, finally, to a reunion. For Ron and Roger, as for Alice and Jack, a series of unbelievable Godwinks strengthened their faith and lifted their hopes.

For my thoughts are not your thoughts,
neither are your ways my ways, declares the LORD.
—ISAIAH 55:8 NIV

3

There's a Bigger Picture Than What You Can See

There's no such thing as chance.
And what to us seems merest accident
Springs from the deepest source of destiny.
Johann von Schiller

Things would look different to us if we could see them from a higher perspective. We are sometimes frustrated that we can see only one piece of the jigsaw puzzle of our life at a time, and we wonder, at crossroads in our lives, how this odd-looking piece fits into the completed puzzle.

Imagine you're a child again. You're on a treasure hunt. You have a quest to discover the Godwinks that have occurred throughout your life, particularly at crossroads.

On this treasure hunt into your own past, don't give up. Rediscovering your dismissed, repressed, and long-forgotten Godwinks requires perseverance. You know, of course, that everything good requires effort. Good diet and exercise lead to better health. Homework and study prepare you for your profession or avocation. And your effort to recall your Godwinks will give you renewed hope for the future as well as new confidence about where you are going, because you will more clearly see how God has been erecting signposts—winking directly at you—all along your life's path.

Twenty years later, the "Aha!"

Take the story of Barbra Streisand and James Brolin. Years before they met and fell in love, there was a Godwink that carried no meaning whatsoever until they looked back two decades later and were able to see the bigger picture of their lives.

A few weeks before their wedding, they were comparing unusual Godwinks that had happened to them. That's when Brolin revealed an incident which had occurred many years earlier when he was looking for an apartment in New York City.

"I had been trudging around for days, and every apartment started looking just like the last one," he said. "Then I walked into this one apartment and immediately had the feeling that *this* was it—this was really right for me."

The broker later told Brolin he was lucky he had gotten it.

"Barbra Streisand had just been in that apartment," he confided. "She loved it, said it was perfect, but because it was a hot day and there was no air conditioning, she wanted time to think about it."

The couple was struck by the fact that, without knowing it, they had been on paths that seemed destined to intersect. The power of that Godwink, revealed long after the fact and on the brink of a major commitment, provided a comforting confirmation for them. "It was a sign helping us in our decision to marry," said Barbra.

Our view of life is limited. We go from day to day, looking at one puzzle piece at a time. But there is another perspective. While we are trying to make sense out of one odd-looking piece after another, we can take comfort knowing that all of the pieces *do* fit into a plan that could only have been created by God. Only when we near the finish and begin to attain a more global perspective does the whole composition have clarity.

When someone in a car ahead of you is killed in a freak accident, you may ask, "Why him, not me?" Yet like other unexpected, undesirable, or uncontrollable fateful detours in your life, death may, in fact, be a graduation to a better place. Graduations are bittersweet because they are crossroads in life. Crossroads represent change. And change produces uncertainty about the future. Although you can't see into the comforts of the future, you can look for the Godwinks when you're at a point of traumatic change.

On the other hand, at times of uncertainty, there's an underlying hope that the unknown will foster *greater* certainty, happiness, and peace. In Beth Wilkensen's story that follows you'll see living proof of this statement.

Out of despair comes . . .

Beth couldn't stop sobbing.

Just two days earlier, things had seemed so good—her father's heart transplant appeared to have been successful.

Then the 6 A.M. phone call: Dad had died. Please come home. She quickly arranged a flight and dashed to the New Orleans airport.

At her gate was just one solitary jean-clad man, reading the paper.

As she waited for her flight, tears streamed down her cheeks. Her dad was too young to die—only fifty-nine. He had been getting better. It wasn't fair for him to be taken so soon. What would she do without him? She was lost in her grief.

Suddenly, a comforting hand was on her shoulder. The voice was warm and oddly familiar. "Are you all right?" It was the man in the jeans. Speaking with him seemed natural—he was nice, and he was concerned about her loss. And there was a sense that she had known him before.

"You're Kevin Costner," she blurted, as it came to her.

He smiled and nodded. He explained that he was in New Orleans scouting for an upcoming film, *JFK*, and was waiting for a private plane.

They chatted. He comforted her, placing an arm around her shoulder like a brother, staying with her until her plane

24

arrived, and waving off advisors who came to tell him his plane was ready, until the time came for him to walk her to the jetway.

"I'll be back in New Orleans in a couple of months for the shoot. Come by the set and see how a movie is made," he smiled. And then, taking her hand, Kevin looked into Beth's eyes and said, "Please tell your mom that I am sorry for her loss—and tell her that good things always come from sad times."

To this day, Beth's mom believes that God was speaking through Kevin Costner.

Two months later, Beth was juggling her final studies for an MBA while working in the financial department of a New Orleans hospital. She had some legal papers that had to get out that day, and she needed to mail them from a post office clear across town, near Lafitte Historical Park.

Driving past the park, she noticed trucks used for movie making. She recalled Kevin Costner at the airport, comforting her and inviting her to visit the set of the film. The notion crossed her mind that perhaps *that* was Kevin's movie. But she had work to do, and so she carried on.

Returning from the post office, she passed Lafitte Park again. This time she hesitated, thinking that, after all, it was late afternoon—no point returning to the office. She stopped and approached a security person, who confirmed that the film in production was indeed *JFK*.

"Would you please tell Kevin that the sobbing woman from the airport is here?"

Kevin smiled broadly when the security person spoke with him, looked up, and waved her over. He greeted her warmly, gave her a place to sit, and told her that someone would come by to stay with her. Moments later, Beth noticed a handsome, well-tanned man approaching.

"He's the best-looking thing I've ever seen," she said to herself.

Roger Armstrong introduced himself as the film's public-relations executive. They chatted quietly as the actors and crew went about their work, and Roger explained what was going on.

That evening on the phone, Beth told her mother with firm finality, "Today I met the man I'm going to marry."

Beth returned to the set several times over the next few weeks—ostensibly to see how movies are made and say hello to Kevin Costner, but in reality to see Roger.

One afternoon Kevin invited them to watch a basketball game on television in his dressing room. Beth took the opportunity to ask Roger if he would like to go out for dinner.

"Sure, when?"

"How about tonight?"

It was an evening of instant confirmation—they were soul mates.

Several weeks later Roger called Beth from the film's

next shooting location and told her he missed her. He convinced her to move to Los Angeles. Eight months later, they were married.

As a postscript, Beth later asked her husband what he would like to be doing if he hadn't become a public-relations executive. He explained that he had kind of fallen into the PR job and had risen rapidly, becoming a twenty-four-year-old vice president at Universal, and then with Tri-Star. He had become much too successful to stop and to do what he always *wanted* to do: become a lawyer.

Beth urged him to look at things differently. She was making a good salary, she reasoned, so why not go for it?

Today Beth and Roger have a young child; Roger is a successful entertainment lawyer, and Beth is the chief financial officer for a private school. Not long ago, when Kevin Costner introduced Beth and Roger to someone, he said, smiling proudly, claiming the role of matchmaker, "I brought them together."

On the day of her father's death, Beth could never have seen how this very sorrowful piece of her life's puzzle would change her life in a positive way. Not only did the puzzle piece that was her father's death help her fill in the rest of her life's picture and find happiness, it also set off a chain of events that gave Roger the encouragement he needed to pursue his dream.

One puzzle piece, two lives affected forever.

What turning points in your life were accompanied by winks from above? Can you see the comfort you've been getting—the reassurance that you are a child of God and that He is looking out for you?

> *I know the plans I have for you . . .*
> *plans to give you hope and a future.*
> —JEREMIAH 29:11 NIV

4

Trust in Your Dreams and Possibilities

Shoot for the moon, and the worst that can happen,
you'll land among the stars.
Tony Orlando

All things are possible. This statement is true, of course, only when you believe it.

The following story is of determination and grit and of the power of belief in oneself, a belief that grew to Olympian proportions.

Mary Lou Retton reflected, "The first time I really began dreaming about the Olympics was in 1976 when Nadia Comaneci won her three gold medals. I was eight years old that summer, and I remember lying on the living-room floor back home in Fairmont, West Virginia, watching the whole thing on television."

After those Olympics, Mary Lou got busy. She enrolled in gymnastics classes, building on her natural attributes and abilities: muscular thighs, explosive runs, and fearlessness. The thought of being a champion like Nadia provided the impetus to grind away at gymnastics for hours, despite turned ankles, sprained wrists, or dislocated fingers. She would say to herself, "Mary Lou, you're going to be in the 1984 Olympics. You'll be sixteen, in your prime."

At fourteen, she convinced her parents to allow her to move to Houston to train with Nadia's legendary coach, Bela Karolyi. Her workouts were harder than before. "No, no, no!" Karolyi would thunder repeatedly.

His tough and sometimes unforgiving coaching style was too much for some gymnasts. But because of her own unswerving faith in herself, it worked with Mary Lou, enabling her to be the best she could.

But there was another obstacle in her path: time.

Time was against her. She had very little national track record, no visibility, and a limited standing with the U.S. Olympic Committee. And the 1984 Olympics were looming. No matter how hard Karolyi tried to focus the committee's attention on Mary Lou, he received only a bureaucratic cold shoulder. She was an unknown; why should they bother?

Mary Lou didn't let their indifference deter her.

In 1983, the America Cup at Madison Square Garden in New York was the last chance to gain some attention before the 1984 Olympics. Without prior approval from the committee, Coach Karolyi decided to take Mary Lou along as an alternate. And even with no certain chance for her to compete, he worked her harder than the other teammates.

She was prepared for the Godwink. It came.

One of the American contenders was unable to compete. Here was Mary Lou's chance to show the world—and the U.S. Olympic Committee—what she had known all along that she could do.

That afternoon she dazzled them at Madison Square Garden. She won the America Cup and instantly gained the necessary attention and respect to be included on the U.S. Olympic roster.

Only a few months later, Mary Lou Retton was on the floor, facing the vault, in the final minutes of the gymnastics competition at the Los Angeles Summer Olympics. Nine years of training had come down to four seconds.

Her lips were tightened with determination. This was her last chance. Her explosive sprint and flawless vault, not once but twice, scored perfect tens. Mary Lou's arms shot up in jubilation even before the scoreboard announced the results. Her smile captivated the world.

A reporter said, "There had never been a moment remotely like it in gymnastics history. An American teenager who'd been on her national team for only fourteen months had won the Olympic all-around title by five one-hundredths of a point, by nailing her last two routines for perfect scores."

They ignored her. They told her she couldn't. Her coach was the toughest there is. But Mary Lou Retton refused to be awestruck by those in authority. She knew her abilities, and more important, she would not give up on her dream.

Mary Lou Retton had become America's first gold medalist in women's gymnastics.

That's the power of trusting in dreams and possibilities. Now it's your turn!

Ten Steps to Success

Inspired by my hero Norman Vincent Peale and the principles he wrote in his book, *The Power of Positive Thinking*, I have devised the following ten-step strategy to help you to map the best possible course on the highway to your destiny. Practice these ten steps daily, and I promise you that your dreams will be closer and your life will be better.

1. *See yourself succeeding!* Formulate a mental picture of yourself being successful. Be as specific as you can, picturing the setting, what you're wearing, who else is present, and what you're saying and doing. Hold on to that picture with bulldog tenacity. Don't let it fade. Keep looking at it every day. Your mind will try to complete what it pictures. So only picture yourself succeeding, never failing.

Take that successful picture of yourself and put it to paper in your wink diary. The simple act of giving birth to the image of "the successful you" on paper will help to create the *you* in your dreams. Believe it will happen!

2. *Cancel negative contractions—can't, won't, don't!* Whenever a negative contraction comes to mind, immediately cancel it out. Focus on the picture you drew of yourself succeeding and say positively, "I can! I will! I do!"

3. *Deflate your obstacles and wipe away trouble!* When your obstacles seem fearfully large and looming, let the air out of them! Fear and worry are nothing more tangible than hot air. *Pssst.* They're gone!

When a problem arises, deal with it in an unemotional, rational way. Refuse to give it any more power than it deserves. Imagine that problem to be a drop of rain hitting your windshield. Turn on the wipers, and watch it disappear!

What is in your way? Draw it in your wink diary. Go ahead. It's OK if it looks ridiculous, because it's hard to be fearful of something ridiculous. Once you've drawn this picture, then draw it again—this time, deflated. Let out the hot air and take away the power of your obstacle.

From now on, whenever you see this obstacle, either in person or in your mind, substitute the deflated picture you just drew.

4. *Don't be awestruck by others—model them!* Try to learn from and emulate the strengths you see in others. Instead of viewing their accomplishments as a reflection on your lack of achievement, use them as a model for your own success.

5. *Find a coach!* Enlist the help of someone with whom you can entrust your self-doubts. By asking them to help you bring your inner ghosts of inferiority to the surface, you will see those doubts and slay them.

6. *Inventory what's good about you!* Trust in yourself and the things about *you* that are desirable and valuable to others. Formulate a nonegoistic yet confident inner love for your own talents and attributes. You can't expect others to love your good qualities if *you* don't.

Make a list in your wink diary of ten good qualities about you that you want others to admire.

7. *Perceive yourself as you wish others to perceive you!* Your very own actions will cue others to the perceptions you wish to have them hold of you. For example, when you speak enthusiastically, conserve words, and walk briskly, others will perceive you as a go-getter. The opposite actions—mumbling slowly and walking in a slouch—will produce the opposite perceptions about you.

Think about the last time you voted for president. Didn't you consciously or unconsciously ask, "Which candidate *looks* the more *presidential*?" If you want others to perceive you as a president, vice president, or manager, start by acting as if you *already are*.

In your wink diary, list ten perceptions that you want others to have about you.

8. *Get the "imp" out of impossible!* Instead, read it as *"I'm possible!"* By getting off your duff and taking small steps, every goal can be reached no matter how difficult it appears. Every mountain climber makes the ascent one small toehold at a time. So, go ahead. Take a step.

9. *Let go, and let God!* You have a powerful ally in every challenge you face. Loosen your grip on those fears which suggest that *you* have to be solely in charge of your challenge. Let your ally help you with it. Let go, and let God.

10. *Look for Godwinks!* The highway pointing toward what you believe to be your destiny may occasionally seem dark and lonely. But you are never alone. Get going, and start looking for the confirming signs that you *are* on the right path. You'll soon see the Godwinks—the "coincidences" and answered prayers—reaffirming that your life is being directed by a super global positioning system.

Follow these ten steps, every day, and you *will* sense that you are heading in the right direction, that you *are* on God's radar screen, and you *will* see the Godwinks of confirmation along your path.

You're now psychologically prepared for the next section of this book: how to use Godwinks to enrich your life and how to turn your wishes into winks.

> *Whether you turn to the right or to the left,*
> *your ears will hear a voice behind you, saying,*
> *"This is the way; walk in it."*
>
> —Isaiah 30:21 NIV

Part Two

Using Godwinks to Enrich Your Life

5

Wishes and Winks

Star light, star bright,
First star I see tonight.
Wish I may, wish I might,
Have the wish I wish tonight.

As a child, you trusted that every wish uttered into a sparkling nighttime sky would come true; you had the clarity to see possibilities, unencumbered by rational thought. You were able to trust in the future without reservation.

At what age did you conclude that wishes were merely childish things? Who told you to "grow up" and robbed you of your dreams?

Let's reclaim your childhood faith in wishes, and let's take it one step further to believe in yourself. Believe that if you wish for something, it can happen. Believe that you *can* be the "somebody" you wished you could be. Believe that you *can* change something about yourself that doesn't satisfy you.

When it comes to wishes, maybe it's time to *stop being such a grownup*, time to return to that state of mind when imagination allowed you the absolute freedom to ask for the impossible, the impractical, and the inconceivable. As adults, we call it prayer, visualization, or focus. But from a childlike mind-set, it's just wishing.

There is a powerful correlation between wishes and winks, because when your wish comes true or your prayer is answered, it sometimes comes in the form of a wink from God.

Here's a case in point. A former actress I know, a widow, was having a hard time. Her husband's life-insurance proceeds had run out, and she couldn't get a job. Her teenagers were growing out of their clothes and the cupboard was empty.

One morning she assessed her situation. The rent was overdue for $550. Her electricity would be shut off unless she paid $44. The phone company was breathing down her neck for a payment of $31.

That meant she needed $625. Her checkbook showed a balance of $24.

My friend didn't have much. But she still had the power of prayer. Before she went into town to run some errands, she took her Bible from the shelf, placed it on the floor, and stood on it. "Lord, you've said to stand on your word and you'll supply all our needs. Well, here I am."

Then she stepped down off her Bible and went on her way.

At the post office her heart leapt. Two letters fell from the junk mail. One held a $310 residual check from an old commercial she had no idea was still running; the other, a $75 refund from a college to which her son had applied.

Buoyant with renewed hope, she rushed to deposit the checks at the bank. That's when she received another joyful piece of news: there had been a clerical error—her checkbook balance was not $24, it was $240!

After the deposits, her bank balance stood at $625—the exact amount she needed to pay the rent and the electric and phone bills.

Now, there's a powerful wink! If you were God and wished to get in touch with humans without using a voice, wouldn't you communicate through little miracles and Godwinks?

Your actions foster Godwinks

Free will is yours. You can choose to live up to your potential or you can choose another path. During most of your life's journey, *your* hands are on the wheel. And you can influence your future through prayer, reading the Bible, and obeying God. When you add your own potential and unique gifts to the mix, you will begin to see signs of hope and encouragement—winks from above.

The following stories provide proof. They are about people who put their wishes *out there*, and then exercised their free will, steadily heading in the right direction, keeping the faith both in themselves and in their maker, and staying alert to the guideposts—the Godwinks—along the way.

Wishing in the Color Purple

Oprah had never wanted anything more in her life.

If there was ever to be a movie based on Alice Walker's 1982 book *The Color Purple*, the role of Sofia belonged to *her*. Ever since she had first read the book, and since the first dozen times she had *re-read* the book, Oprah felt like she was integral to it. And when she heard that Steven Spielberg was going to make the movie, she knew she had to be in it.

Acting, however, was not high on her considerable list of skills. She had previously acted only in high school and college plays. As the host of a Chicago television show that had not yet gone national, how in the world could she become visible to Steven Spielberg and get an audition?

God winked.

Unbeknownst to Oprah, Quincy Jones, the famed producer and musician, had acquired the rights to *The Color Purple*. He was the one who had convinced Spielberg to become involved in the film. On a trip through Chicago, Quincy had caught Oprah's show on television and had come to the same conclusion: she was the perfect Sofia. He called the casting people and asked them to contact Oprah for an audition.

Oprah was flabbergasted. But not too flabbergasted to jump at the opportunity. She auditioned, and then—silence. The next two months were incredibly painful. No one called to tell her whether she had done well or badly. The casting agent had simply said, "Don't call us, we'll call you."

She could not conceive of a single thing to do to move herself closer to her goal. Maybe it was her looks, she thought. Maybe she was overweight. Oprah took action. She enrolled in a workout center in hopes that she could quickly take off thirty pounds. She exhausted herself on the track, running and running, wondering what else she could do.

On the track an old spiritual came to mind, "I Surrender All." She began singing it out loud, right as she ran: "I surrender all, I surrender all." She let go. She let God.

He winked again.

A staff member at the center came out to the running track to tell her that there was a telephone call from Hollywood—Steven Spielberg's office.

"Spielberg wanted to see me in Los Angeles the next day," said Oprah, "and I was told, 'If you lose a pound, you could lose the part.'" The part was Sofia, an indomitable woman who was determined to marry a man named Harpo.

"Harpo—that's Oprah spelled backwards," said Oprah. "And to me that was more than a coincidence. It was a sign the part was for me." Not only did Oprah get the role of Sofia, but the release of the movie was perfectly timed: it immediately preceded the national rollout of *The Oprah Winfrey Show*, which went on to become the most successful syndicated talk show launch in the history of television.

And to close the loop of perfect harmony, when Oprah formed a production company to oversee her show and other projects, she gave it an apt name: Harpo Productions.

When you wish for something, you also need to take action yourself—to place yourself in the direction that you wish to go, the direction that you believe to be in alignment with your destiny. Get on the path. Do everything you can do to be prepared <u>for your maker's reply</u> to your wishes and prayers. Then, like Oprah, let go and wait for the Godwink.

The prayer that saved a life

Doctors at Lenox Hill Hospital in New York worked feverishly to save my newborn son, who had been born in cardiac arrest. His own body waste, which he had inhaled while still in the womb, clogged his lungs and made it impossible for him to breathe on his own.

As I prayed over his incubator, I counted eighteen different tubes and wires protruding from his little body. Dials indicated that a respirator was handling 96 percent of his breathing; he was managing only 4 percent on his own.

His chances for survival were extremely limited.

I had committed to being at his side, praying for him around the clock, catching a catnap every three hours or so. I prayed and prayed, asking God to spare his life.

It was 6 A.M. on the second day of my son's life when I noticed him trembling, then convulsing. I yelled for the nurse. She told me I was witnessing a seizure. As she disappeared to summon a doctor, I noticed a dark substance passing through the transparent tubes that came from his lungs. The seizure was helping to expel the blockage to his little lungs.

Within moments I spotted something else that gave me a surge of joy. The dial attributing his breathing to the machine was beginning to drop. My son's *own* breathing was beginning to increase!

By 8:30 A.M., the respirator dial dropped to 45 percent, meaning that 55 percent of my son's breathing was on his own power!

I had witnessed a miracle. I had prayed for my son, Grant, and he was saved. There was damage to his brain—he will always have learning challenges—but he is alive and well, a sweet, smart young man with an enormous capacity to sing hundreds of songs by heart.

That powerful wink from God was a confirmation that

we can wish very deeply for something, ask God for it in prayer, *believe* that it will happen, and it *will* happen.

> *Whatsoever you*
> *shall ask in prayer,*
> *believing, you shall receive.*
> —MATTHEW 21:22 AKJV

Visualizing the picture

From an early age, Bill Clinton felt the pull of politics. He watched the political conventions on television, read historical books, and studied great leaders. He dreamed of his own political future.

An early high point in his quest transpired at sixteen when he was elected senator in an American Legion–sponsored educational exercise. He won the chance to travel with fifty other Arkansas boys to Washington, D.C., to meet members of Congress and visit the White House.

The White House tour provided no assurance that the boys would get even a glimpse of President John F. Kennedy, let alone have their pictures taken with him. But that's what was on Bill Clinton's mind. One of the trip's chaperones recalled, years later, that Clinton was "bound and determined," long before they began the trip, to have his picture taken with the president.

On the day of the tour, Clinton managed to sit in the

first seat on the bus so that when he and the others filed off and were led into the White House Rose Garden, he'd be in the best position to see the president, in case that were possible.

The spot he had selected was alongside one of two paths the president could use to enter the Rose Garden from the Oval Office. Unfortunately, President Kennedy usually chose the other path.

But that day, God winked more than once.

That morning, the president had read about the Arkansas boys' visit in the morning edition of the *Washington Post* and came out to greet them. He spoke a few words and turned to walk back to the Oval Office. Then, for some reason, he reversed himself, moving back in Clinton's direction. That was precisely the Godwink that Bill Clinton had been waiting for. He stepped forward and thrust out his hand to the president just as an American Legion photographer—another wink from God—was snapping a picture.

These Godwinks from above didn't happen in a vacuum. They happened because Bill Clinton had a dream, a vision, and focused so intensely on it that he actually positioned himself to receive God's messages of hope and encouragement.

The picture of a young Bill Clinton confidently shaking hands with the president of the United States in the Rose Garden was appealing to the Arkansas newspapers. They ran it prominently, and it helped to solidify an image of a young man with a vision—a vision that carried him all the way to his own two terms as president of the United States.

Wish for your own winks

Now *you* try it. Make a wish. Allow yourself a childlike leap to the vision of your future. You have the power within *yourself* to allow Godwinks to happen to you. Here are some questions to ponder:

1. When you were young and wished upon a star, what was your desire? Did someone in your family or school deride you, saying you were just a dreamer? It's time to erase the negative tape in your mind that has been playing those thoughts over and over. Erase it, and replace it with a positive recording—that your childhood wishes *are* possible. Write it in your wink diary. Communicate it to God in prayer.

2. Right here and now, what would you really like to see yourself doing in life? In other words, what do you wish for? What is your dream? Don't hold back by listening to those voices who told you to "be realistic." Write it down, in rich, reach-for-the-stars detail.

3. Now look at the inventory of your abilities that you made in the last chapter. It contains clues to your destiny. As you've accumulated these talents, skills,

and abilities throughout your life, you have been quietly preparing yourself for your dreams all along. Now, write ways you can use those abilities to move toward your dreams. For example, what sorts of careers excite you and require your special set of skills? What type of people mesh best with your personality strengths? Name three ways you can put yourself in a position to step into those careers and meet those sorts of people.

4. Who have you always wanted to meet? All it takes is research to find out where they are going to be—and the gumption to become visible to them. Frequently we roadblock ourselves by saying, "Oh, they are too busy to speak with someone as unimportant as me." The fact is, most people are flattered that someone wants to meet them. Write down the name of the person you'd most like to meet—perhaps a contact who can land you a job in the field you enjoy, the person whose life you admire and wish to learn from. Name three steps you can take to spend some time with that person.

Copy your list and post it somewhere you can see it every day—the refrigerator door, the bathroom mirror—and then believe that as long as you are moving toward your destiny, somewhere, sometime, there'll be a Godwink that will show up like a neon signpost in the fog, confirming that you are on the right path.

Like Bill Clinton, who took initiatives and had faith that he could achieve his desired outcome, you can use your dreams as the first step to creating your own Godwinks.

You can count on it.

> *Everything is possible for one who believes.*
> —MARK 9:23 NIV

6

Take Steps on Your Path to Your Destiny

*We are not permitted to choose
the frame of our destiny.
But what we put into it is ours.*
Dag Hammarskjöld

In the last chapter, we talked about focusing on your objectives and outcomes. You have visualized what you want to happen. Now, while holding that thought firmly in mind, start taking small steps. Without wasting a moment's energy worrying about all the things that might block your path, continue to see yourself at your goal, and keep taking those small steps.

You may think, "What happens if I get off my path, and nothing seems to be going right?" Well, standing by the road kicking your tires in frustration and blaming others—even if they *are* at fault—will not get you closer to your goal. Do what you would do if you were lost on a real highway. Keep moving. Or go back, maybe an exit or two, and re-read the road signs, reorient yourself, and start anew.

Brave steps of faith produce Godwinks

My wife, actress and comedic impressionist Louise DuArt, was truly astounded by the series of Godwinks that emerged when she looked back at her career.

She had wanted to be in show business since childhood. A career as an entertainer was her most fervent wish. So, even though she was extremely shy, she took initiative. She started walking down the path to her destiny, taking the steps needed to place herself in the path of Godwinks. As you read her story, you'll see that at every turning point in her career, a Godwink occurred to let her know she was on the right path.

Wink 1. When she was just starting out, Louise appeared in a show at Los Angeles City College. An agent in the audience was impressed with her performance and came backstage to meet her. Producers Sid and Marty Krofft were searching for a comedienne to replace Billy Hayes in the role of Witchiepoo for the stage version of the *H.R. Pufnstuf* television series. Would she like to audition?

An audition was arranged, but Louise was worried that she'd be too scared to actually perform. So, creating a safety net for herself, she made an audiotape that mimicked Billy Hayes's lines from the television show.

When Louise arrived at the Krofft brothers' office, she nervously asked if she could begin by playing the audiotape. Sid Krofft was befuddled. But he consented.

"Hey," he blurted, "that's Billy Hayes. Why are you playing that?"

"It only sounds like Billy Hayes," Louise responded. "That's me."

She got the job. So an agent who happened to see her performance and happened to know of a perfect role for her was wink number one—and her first career turning point.

Wink 2. This is where I entered the picture. I saw *H.R. Pufnstuf* at Madison Square Garden with my daughters. When Louise burst on stage as Witchiepoo, with a green face and a long warty nose, she commanded attention. Who was this woman?

I was Vice President of Children's Television at ABC and was developing a television series with the Krofft brothers. It involved a rock band called Kaptain Kool and the Kongs, and we had been looking for a comedienne for one of the roles. I suggested the woman who played Witchiepoo in the Kroffts' own stage show—even though she'd had no television experience.

The same forces that placed me in the audience to see Louise DuArt as Witchiepoo provided the bridge to her joining Kaptain Kool and the Kongs and her entry into television. Later that year, the group was so popular that they showed up on the cover of *Newsweek*.

Wink 3. Louise ended up performing in several shows

produced by the Krofft brothers. One show called for a Cher impersonator, who at the last minute couldn't make it. The Kroffts were in trouble. The show was about to go on the air.

"I can do Cher," Louise volunteered to Marty Krofft.

She did. She saved the day, and that experience paved the way for her to become a world-class impressionist. Her roster of more than one hundred dead-on impressions includes Barbra Streisand, Kathie Lee Gifford, Barbara Walters, Judge Judy, Fran Drescher, and even men, such as one-hundred-year-old George Burns.

One wonders, would Louise's career as an impressionist have started if it hadn't been for the Godwink that the Cher impersonator hadn't shown up?

Wink 4. After her two sons were born, Louise put her career on hold for seven years. Then came another turning point. Her husband lost his job.

She decided to return to work herself, but several years of being out-of-sight, out-of-mind in the entertainment business is deadly; she worried that all her old contacts had forgotten her.

Louise's neighborhood friends, who had come to love her wacky voices and sense of humor, urged her to try a comedy act. But she had never created material for an act, she argued; she had only done roles on stage and voices in television shows, commercials, and cartoons. But on a dare from the neighbors, Louise put together seven minutes of impressions and went to a comedy club on open-mike night.

Unbeknownst to Louise, producers for the talent program *Star Search* happened to be showcasing some other talent at the club that night, and by divinely aligned timing, Louise went on just ahead of them. The *Star Search* people loved her and signed her up. Within weeks, she was seen coast-to-coast on television.

Wink 5. Wink five came when Donna Summer was flipping through channels at the very moment Louise was on *Star Search*. Summer had been looking for an opening act for her road tour—someone with a clean comedic routine, compatible with the tone she wanted for her show.

Suddenly, Louise was propelled from everyday mom to a marquee with Donna Summer, who was then one of the hottest singers of the '80s. The tour lasted two years.

Wink 6. In 1991, Louise traveled to New York to promote her upcoming Showtime television special on *Good Morning America*. While there, she and a friend took in a show, *Catskills on Broadway*. The show starred four comics who had honed their talents in New York's Catskill Mountain resorts: Freddie Roman, Dick Capri, Mal Z. Lawrence, and impressionistic-singer Marilyn Michaels.

Right from the start of the performance, Louise was overcome with an odd, exciting feeling. There was something about the show that was very special. Afterwards at Sardi's famous theater-district restaurant, she confided to her friend "I'm going to do this show."

The friend smiled.

But Louise's instincts were prophetic, because moments later, someone sent drinks to their table. "From whom?" she asked the waiter.

"The gentlemen behind you," he nodded. Seated at the very next table were the three male stars of *Catskills on Broadway*.

Freddie Roman broke into a big smile, reminding Louise that they had once been on the same talk show. "You won't believe this, Louise, but I was just talking about you. I told these guys that if Marilyn Michaels ever leaves the show, I know the perfect person. You. But I didn't know how to reach you. Then I look up and there you are!"

Two weeks later, Louise got a call: "Marilyn's leaving. How would you like to star in *Catskills on Broadway?*"

This was a defining moment in her career.

But in the midst of the turning point, Louise ran into roadblocks. Her business managers told her she was crazy; salaries for Broadway actors are typically a fraction of those for television and touring performers. Her mother and her neighbors begged her not to go, citing that her roots were now in Los Angeles.

Everyone seemed to have a logical argument. Yet the

extraordinary Godwink of meeting the *Catskills* comics at Sardi's, at the very moment they were talking about recruiting *her* for the show, was a sign too powerful to ignore. More than anything else, that auspicious meeting convinced Louise that God was giving her a wink.

Against everyone's advice except God's, Louise took the job and began a whole new chapter in her life. Playing a starring role on Broadway turned out to be a great boost and career crossroads.

Wink 7. After she had performed for one year in *Catskills on Broadway*, Louise's husband, who was also her manager, provided one more turning point. He asked for a divorce. She remembers the date because it was the same day on which her father had passed away one year before: November 13.

Later, when she could see the bigger picture, Louise realized that the divorce was a blessing in disguise; she found that her life was happier, and she hired a manager who better bolstered her career. On reflection, she concluded that the significance of the death of her marriage on the anniversary of her father's death was a strong message to maintain her faith that everything would turn out OK.

When we lay out the trail of Godwinks that have guided Louise's life, we can see that His signposts were there at every turning point. Every wink was a powerful reassurance that she was going in the right direction.

Go ahead—take some steps!

Like Louise did, once you've articulated your dream, it's time to act. Do you remember that picture you drew of yourself succeeding? Well, it's time to start bringing it into real-life, three-dimensional living color. Some people call the steps you need to take to live your dream "networking" or "career development." Whatever you call them, one thing is for sure: it will be hard work.

But it's your life and it's your work! Aren't you worth it?

When you're out there doing the hard work of making your wishes come true, you'll have periods when nothing seems to be happening. Don't stop! The Godwinks are coming, and all the preparation you've been doing is getting you ready to recognize them. And when they do come, you'll have the reassurance you need that you're on the right path.

Get going!

> *Let us not become weary in doing good,*
> *for at the proper time we will reap a harvest*
> *if we do not give up.*
>
> —GALATIANS 6:9 NIV

7

Reflect on and Take Comfort
from Godwinks

*All I have seen teaches me to trust
the creator for all I have not seen.*
Ralph Waldo Emerson

Sometimes when we're troubled by rough spots in our lives, it seems as though nothing can soothe our anxious mind. Expensive counseling sessions, long talks with friends, or even inspirational books like this don't seem to address our specific state of disharmony. That's how Allison and Judy felt in the following stories. What finally brought them both to a peaceful place was their own openness—God winked at them, and both were receptive enough to take notice and to take comfort.

Who is that man?

Sixteen-year-old Allison was thumbing through an old photo album with her new stepfather, Robert Applegate. Divorce and remarriage are difficult for every child, particularly teenagers, and Allison was still trying to resolve the conflict between her mind and her heart. Intellectually she was happy for her mom, who was clearly more joyful since her new marriage. She was also happy for her dad in his new life. And she loved her new stepfather.

But down deep, she couldn't help but feel a sense of loss that her mom and dad couldn't still be together and that they couldn't still be the happy family she remembered, as evidenced in photo after photo of happy holidays, playful shots of Allison's first pony ride, and fun-filled family trips together.

Allison politely narrated each picture, identifying person after person for her stepfather. She paused to smile at a "Kodak moment" from years before: she was five, and her parents had taken her to the Bahamas. She and Robert giggled at her face, covered with spaghetti sauce, while dining in a restaurant with her mom and dad.

Suddenly, Allison saw something in the picture she had never noticed before—a man seated at the table right behind theirs. "Hey! That looks like you!" she exclaimed.

"You're right, it does," said Robert, bending closer to the picture. "That *is* me. Look at the date of the picture. I was also in the Bahamas at that time!"

Within moments, the power of the Godwink registered with Allison. Nine years before her mother met and married Robert Applegate, Allison's family of the future was divinely placed at *adjacent* tables on an island thousands of miles away. It was a wink that in a flash brought an inner peace to Allison, a confirming sign that everything was going to be just fine.

Home is where the heart is

For Judy Bishop, an extraordinary Godwink marked a significant turning point in her life. She was attending a bridal shower in New York City. After spending the evening with her friend, who was glowing with the prospect of a happy marriage, Bishop was feeling somewhat remorseful about her own marriage as she left the gathering. She had a long drive ahead to her home in New Jersey, and while walking to her parked car on West 80th Street at West End Avenue, she stopped to wistfully look into a window. Inside was a warm, inviting home, an apartment with high ceilings and a lot of plants. "That's where I should be," Bishop thought to herself.

With those thoughts in mind, Bishop decided the following week to sell her house in the country and move into the city.

She picked up the *New York Times* and found the telephone number of a real-estate broker, who met her at his office in New York that very afternoon. She was stunned that the first apartment on his list was on West 80th Street right near West End Avenue.

But she was totally floored when they arrived at the

building. It was the *very* apartment she had wistfully looked into and said, "That's where I should be." Unable to ignore a Godwink of that magnitude, she moved in and lived there for many years.

Now, just ask yourself: How many apartments are there in New York City? Don't bother counting. It's a *lot*. Let's just agree: Judy Bishop had every right to be astonished by the remarkable Godwink at that fragile moment in her life.

That wink gave her a new sense of confidence in herself and an assurance that she was not alone.

Sometimes life is challenging. Things seem to be out of our control. But how we choose to respond to life is up to us. We can choose to look for and remain open to God's comforting winks and move ahead, confident that we are part of His plan, or we can ignore the Godwinks from above and lose heart.

It seems unwise to ignore a source of comfort. Isn't it much better to acknowledge the life-affirming nature of Godwinks, which assure us that we are not alone?

A wink of compassion

The Kennedys are an American family that has experienced tragedies of Shakespearean proportions. They suffered, generation after generation. For those of us watching for the Godwinks, even in tragedy, some comfort can be taken.

On July 16, 1999, John F. Kennedy Jr.; his wife, Caroline; and her sister, Laura Bissette, were killed when their small plane plummeted from hazy nighttime skies into the Atlantic Ocean, seven miles west of Martha's Vineyard. Five days later, their bodies were recovered. They were buried at sea the next day, July 22. The nation watched as family and friends attended memorial services.

How many times did you whisper to yourself, "Why? Why would three young people be taken so suddenly?" Yet several extraordinary Godwinks comforted those who took note. At various times during the week after the crash, one Godwink after another was signaled as reporters began their news stories with the word "Ironically."

- Ironically, when searching for JFK Jr.'s plane, the Coast Guard Search and Rescue Teams combed the same waters where, three years to the day, TWA Flight 800 had disappeared.
- Ironically, exactly thirty years prior to that weekend, John F. Kennedy Jr.'s uncle, Senator Edward Kennedy, drove his car off Chappaquiddick Bridge on Martha's Vineyard, taking the life of the young woman riding with him.
- Ironically, Stanley Tretick, 77, the White House photographer who took the famous photo of toddler John F. Kennedy Jr. peeking from beneath his father's

desk in the Oval Office, died on the third day of the search.

- Ironically, John F. Kennedy Jr.'s identification papers washed ashore onto the beach directly in line with his own property at Martha's Vineyard.
- Ironically, just prior to taking his fateful trip, Kennedy was editing a story for his magazine, *George*, featuring actor Harrison Ford promoting a movie about a man whose small plane crashed at sea.

As terrible as this tragedy seemed, the winks from God were messages of reassurance dispatched to the rest of us to bolster our faith in God's greater plan. For while we ask, "Why would God take those young lives?" we must remind ourselves that we are seeing only a small piece of the puzzle—that there is a *whole* picture, and we all fit into it.

A person's way of life is not his own;
no one who walks determines his own steps.
—JEREMIAH 10:23 CSB

Part Three

Godwinks in All Walks of Life

8

Relationship Godwinks

*Life is a flower of which
love is the honey.*
Victor Hugo

Relationships. Your perfect mate—if not already in your life—is out there waiting for you. In the web of life, you are holding an invisible strand of love which is held at the other end by the mate who is intended for you. Trust in yourself, and watch for the Godwinks that direct you to the person at the other end of your strand.

It doesn't happen overnight. Sometimes God's guideposts are small winks, and sometimes they're in your face. But you'll never see them if you're concealing yourself in fear of being rejected or hurt. It's up to you to actively look for the signs and to consciously consider their meaning when they do appear.

If you're like most people, you sail along your stream of life paying scant attention to the tributaries that merge other people into and out of your existence. Well, start giving them more deference: These are the people who are unwittingly placed in your path by divine alignment and are part of your life's greater plan.

Sometimes a person you encounter creates a turning point, sending your life in a whole new direction. If you are alert, you will recognize the Godwinks at these turning points—confirming that you're going in the right direction.

Just such a moment is when you meet your future soul mate.

"How did you two meet?" That's an age-old question which most people have heard at one time or another. I suspect you also have a story or two about times when you met someone and thought you were in love. But if you recall seeing no signs—no Godwinks—then perhaps it was His way of saying that you were *not* on the right path. Perhaps that wasn't your perfect relationship.

One thing is certain: People who have found their perfect partners—their soul mates—attest that the turning point in their relationship was accompanied by clear and powerful Godwinks.

As you consider the circumstances of the couples in the following stories, think about your own relationships. Can you remember a time you were dating someone and may have overlooked the tuner GPS confirming winks from your God's Positioning System?

A spiritual awakening

In 1988, Shira Monast had turned thirty-one and felt deeply motivated to search for her *Bashert*, her "intended one." In Hebrew, *Bashert* is a term that carries a deeper meaning than *soul mate*. Perhaps her compulsion to travel to Israel from her home in the American Southwest reflected a need to seek spiritual guidance. She was not sure.

In July, Shira visited Israel's ancient city of Svfad. At a folk-art shop, an artist looked at her closely. "I have something for you," he said, disappearing into the back of the shop. Returning, he handed her a copper etching unlike most of his other work—a picture of an unbearded man with a receding hairline, hugging a woman and a child. The artist had drawn rays of light around the man, giving him a sacred appearance.

At first, Shira tried to give it back or at least to pay for it. But the shop owner refused. "This is for you" was all he would say.

After she returned from Israel, Shira's quest to find her niche—and her *Bashert*—seemed to pull her to New York City. She took up temporary residence on the Lower East Side. In November 1988, a postcard came to the address at which she was living. Picking it up, Shira wondered how her name could have gotten on anyone's mailing list in so short a time. The postcard said there would be a gathering on Saturday, December 3, for Sabbath services and the first meeting of a *havurah* at a Park Avenue address. A *havurah* is a fellowship circle designed to help Jews find a more meaningful connection to the Torah.

Jeffrey Reiss should have been at peace. He was enviously successful. His life was materially rich—yet spiritually barren. Prior to attending a gathering in December 1987 at which a rabbi rattled Jeffrey's perception of religion, he had considered himself an atheist. Afterwards, he was simply confused.

Subsequently, for the entire next year, 1988, he was drawn to the study of Judaism, while his life, including a relationship with a woman of another faith, drifted without a compass. Strange urgings guided him. He was moved to help a struggling artist who painted haunting images of the Holocaust. He found himself helping another artist, and then another. He was provoked to commit extraordinary time and money to the enhancement of the environment.

In mid-1988, a *havurah* was hosted in Philadelphia by the same rabbi who had triggered Jeffrey's spiritual explorations. The meeting was like a breath of fresh air. "Before today, I felt like I didn't fit into the Jewish community," Jeffrey told the rabbi. "I wish there was something like this in New York."

"Why don't *you* start a *havurah?*" asked the rabbi.

Jeffrey looked at him in disbelief. "I couldn't—I am ignorant about Judaism," he said quietly.

But later, Jeffrey pondered the rabbi's suggestion. "Hosting a *havurah* is a ridiculous idea. It would take a miracle," he argued with himself. "But—if it *were* possible—then I would have to believe in the *maker* of miracles," he conceded.

Over the next few months, Jeffrey inflated his courage and resolved to schedule a fellowship circle at his New York apartment. A mailing list evolved, made up of names acquired from here and there, and postcards were sent out. The date: Saturday, December 3, 1988.

On the eve of the *havurah*, Jeffrey confided to his girlfriend that another odd thing had happened to him: For several weeks, a place he had never visited kept insinuating itself into his consciousness through conversations, in a song on the radio, on a billboard, in a news story. Somehow, he was feeling an inner compulsion to go there.

"Where?"

"New Mexico."

"New Mexico?"

"Yes, Albuquerque, New Mexico."

They stared at each other for a moment before dismissing the idea as absurd.

On the day of the *havurah*, Jeffrey worried that he had not sufficiently put out the word. Perhaps no one will come, he thought. But by 10 A.M., attendance was the least of his worries. His apartment overflowed with sixty people.

That day was a turning point in the life of Jeffrey Reiss. It wasn't until later that the Godwink struck him—it was exactly one year to the day since the meeting at which he had first heard the rabbi speak, commencing his transformation.

The daylong immersion into prayerful soul-searching brought him to tears as he stood before the group sharing the story of his life-changing journey.

Seated among the attendees, Shira Monast looked at the man who was speaking and nudged her companion. "That's him," said Shira in excited, hushed tones.

"Who?" asked her girlfriend.

"He's the man in the copper etching. He looks just like the man embracing the woman and the child—with rays of light shining on him. Look. Even his hairline is the same."

Jeffrey continued speaking to the group, including a story—"coincidentally"—about a vision that once occurred to him in which he was pierced by rays of light. By late afternoon, each of the attendees expressed their thanks to the host for inviting them to such a spiritually awakening experience. The *havurah* was a major success. Among the participants waiting to thank Jeffrey was Shira. She lingered for a moment to compliment the decor of his apartment and inquired if he knew of a place she could rent.

"I'm thinking of moving to New York," she said.

"From where?" he asked.

"Albuquerque, New Mexico," she replied.

Jeffrey was dumbfounded. Then his spirit leaped as he looked into her eyes. "I've always wanted to go there," he blurted.

"Really? I'm going there in two weeks," smiled Shira, flushing with the quiver of deep inner happiness, sensing that one journey was ending as another was about to begin.

"I'll go with you," he said.

"You can't. I'm going on a canoe trip."

"I love canoeing," he lied.

That evening Jeffrey reflected on the day. It was all he had hoped for, and more. He had felt the miracle—the God-wink—that confirmed his belief in the *maker* of miracles. Not only had he pulled off what he had once considered impossible—by hosting the *havurah*—but his intended one—his *Bashert*—was led to the gathering.

That evening Shira phoned her mother. "Today I met my *Bashert*," she confided, "the man I'm going to marry."

The following day Jeffrey invited Shira to dinner, and for hours they talked of the role spirituality played in their lives. They shared their mutual, yearlong search to unravel the meaning of it all. "You know we are *Bashert*," said Jeffrey, matter-of-factly, on the ride back to their meeting place—his apartment. "Yes, I know," said Shira, with quiet confidence. Later, walking around the dining table, Jeffrey imagined aloud, "Can you see us sitting here, having *Shabbos* dinner with our children?"

"Yes, I can," said Shira, reflecting on the etching of a man, embracing a woman and a child, that was given to her by a stranger—an Israeli artist who said, "This is for you."

Two weeks later, Jeffrey traveled to Albuquerque to have dinner with Shira. Eight months after that, they were married. Today, they have two children. The power of the confirming coincidences for Jeffrey and Shira Reiss led them down the unmistakable path toward each other— their *Bashert*.

Recently, Shira added a postscript to her story with Jeffrey. "Just a few days ago, I asked him, 'After twelve years, do you still feel the soul connection?'"

"Yes—without question," he smiled.

"Me too."

Shira and Jeffrey, each holding one end of an invisible strand of love, were tugged inexplicably toward each other by powerful winks from God. An exotic etching that Shira received in Israel turned out to be Jeffrey's likeness; the invitation that Shira mysteriously received to Jeffrey's home was for an event which was divinely aligned on the anniversary of his spiritual awakening; and the thoughts of Albuquerque, New Mexico, invading Jeffrey's consciousness—in hindsight, all were Godwinks, or signposts, leading Shira and Jeffrey to each other.

Food for the soul

The principal players in this story are Maria Zimmitti and Paul Cohn.

Maria was a graduate student, two years into a five-year clinical psychology program at the California School of Professional Psychology, and the only member of a musically talented family who wasn't heading into show business. Having been jaded by an off-again, on-again relationship, she was taking a hiatus from men.

Paul was all the way across the country in Washington, D.C.—twice-married, and twenty-eight years her senior. Moreover, at the moment, Paul was married to his career: he was a successful restaurateur on his way to owning more than a dozen eateries.

What forces of nature could possibly bring them together and cast them as a perfect couple?

Maria's mother, Jonnie—a strong, free-spirited woman— had enthusiastically relocated to D.C., and she invited her daughter to visit the nation's capital. "Maybe you'll meet someone nice here," her mother telephoned.

"Mom, I've done the man thing in L.A.—no thanks."

But in the spring of 1993, the offer of a free plane ticket sounded appealing, especially after a long winter of study.

Picking her up at National Airport, Jonnie and a friend named Keith suggested they go directly to their favorite Georgetown restaurant, Paolo's, for lunch. But it was such a beautiful spring day as they entered Paolo's that Jonnie lobbied for a different choice: "Let's go down by the harbor. There's a wonderful restaurant with tables outside by the water."

It was a five-block walk down to the harbor. Settling in at the new restaurant to order drinks, Keith became irritated. They didn't have his favorite beer. "C'mon, let's go back to Paolo's," he insisted. Disguising their annoyance, Maria and Jonnie reluctantly yielded to his stubbornness and made the trek, five long blocks back up the hill, to Paolo's. By the time they were seated, at 3:30 P.M., the restaurant was sparsely populated.

Owner Paul Cohn spotted his regular customers and approached their table. In introducing Maria, Keith observed that she and Paul had something in common: Maria came from a musical family, and Paul also had a musical past.

"What did you do?" she asked.

"I managed the '70s group Peaches & Herb," answered Paul.

"Really!" said Maria, excitedly. "My father played with Peaches & Herb. He was their percussionist."

"Bob Zimmitti," added Jonnie.

"I know him," said Paul. "I mean, we never met, but Bob Zimmitti is the best percussionist in L.A. He worked with Streisand, the Bee Gees—he's the best."

Before the visit ended, Keith's boldness again prompted Maria and her mother to exchange sidelong glances. He asked Paul to place their names at the door of Paul's new D.C. hot spot, Club Zei, for 10:30 P.M. on Saturday. Paul said he would, adding it was unlikely he would be there; he rarely showed up at Club Zei at that time of night.

But on that Saturday night, Paul found that he had some business at another of his establishments nearby and decided to walk over to Club Zei, just to be certain that their names were on the list. He happened to be standing at the front door just as Keith, Jonnie, and Maria arrived.

As Paul and Maria's eyes met, it was different from their first meeting. This time, the rest of the world seemed to disappear. They began talking, and they didn't stop until the wee hours of the morning. Paul was captivated with Maria—both by her interests and her study of child psychology. They talked about his children from a previous marriage, his marriage to Peaches of Peaches & Herb, and how he'd moved from show business to the showy business of restaurant management. Maria talked about her musical family—her father, brother, and stepmother—and how only she had decided to march to the beat of a different drummer. She talked of former boyfriends and unsatisfying relationships.

They talked and talked, long into the night. And they kept talking. For the next three years of Maria's graduate school in Los Angeles, Paul talked to Maria every single morning—awakening her at 6 A.M.

Maria and Paul never had a doubt. From the very first moment at the nightclub, an abnormal energy entwined their hearts, drew them close, and assured them that they had each found something rarer than gold: their soul mate. With periodic bi-coastal visits, they endured the three years until Maria was able to move to Washington, D.C. Their commitment to each other was commemorated with a small wedding in Sedona, Arizona.

The Godwink of Paul's past with Peaches & Herb— and Maria's father's relationship with the same musical act—was a powerful wink for Paul and Maria, convincing them that they were on the path that would lead them to their life's partner.

By raising your consciousness to the Godwinks in your life, you'll see how you are being led in one direction or another—and that even the littlest things—like a bottle of beer—can be an instrument of those mysterious forces that lead you to your soul mate.

In pursuit of the treasure of love

Finding your perfect relationship is like finding a treasure. But then, discovering most treasure calls for a treasure *hunt*.

And treasure is not easy to find. As I write this, I'm sitting on an airplane next to a woman who told me that she is about to celebrate her first wedding anniversary. "It is so wonderful when you *really* fall in love and—no matter how long you're married—you still feel like you're dating, missing him when he's not with you, and getting a rush of excitement when you see each other again." She added quietly, "I had to look for him for twenty years—it took a lot of patience—but I found him."

Steps to finding your soul mate

There *is* a perfect mate for you. When you see the meticulous perfection in nature, in the perfect symmetry of a flower or in the graceful beauty of a soaring dove, how can you doubt that your life should share in that perfect unified balance of creation?

Here are five steps to take to keep your heart—and your eyes—open to the winks that could lead you to your mate.

1. *Set a positive attitude.* Look around you. When you see a couple that looks happy together, don't they generally look perfectly cast? Don't they usually appear to have compatible looks and comparable temperaments? God loves symmetry. Like the happy couples you see, somewhere there is a perfect mate for you.

2. *Start loving yourself*. Before you can fall in love with someone else—or expect them to fall in love with you—*you* need to fall in love with you. You've made an inventory of the wonderful things about yourself. Now focus your attention on those things, setting aside things you don't like about yourself. Choose activities that highlight your strengths. Adopt a positive impression of who you are, and decide right here and now that *you* are a perfect catch for someone. Write down five activities in your wink diary that would be a good place to showcase you at your most lovable and energetic—five activities at which you shine.

3. *Have faith*. There's no value in being desperate to find your soul mate. Yes, you *do* need to take action, but measured, confident steps, not a frenzied, obsessed search. Believe with all your heart that there will be guideposts for you to follow, but realize that they might not appear on your timetable.

4. *Get on your universal highway*. Start heading in the direction that you believe to be your destiny. You can't get there by sitting by the road waiting for someone to stop. You can't get there by hiding behind your fears that you are not good enough or that no one is there for you. You need to assert yourself. And when you do, you will begin to see the guideposts. Shira Monast took trips to Israel and New

York in search of her *Bashert*. In Israel, the shop-keeper giving her a copper etching of a man who eventually looked just like Jeffrey Reiss, her soul mate, was one guidepost. In New York, the postcard finding her, announcing a fellowship circle hosted by her soul mate, when she had barely arrived in town, was another guidepost. What are three steps you can take, like Shira did, to move you further down the path toward your mate?

5. *Stay alert for the signs to your perfect mate.* There are Godwinks waiting for you. Choose to see winks as meaningful signals that *you* are on the right track. Their occurrence is meant to reassure you. Let them buoy you up so that your best face shines. Even when you haven't yet found your *Bashert*, your intended one, you are never alone.

Remember, people are drawn to the light. When you know your strengths and place yourself in situations where you can shine brightest, you'll be amazed at who notices and how many winks of encouragement you'll receive.

I am the light of the world. Whoever follows me
will not walk in darkness, but will have the light of life.

—JOHN 8:12 ESV

9

Family Godwinks

Sorrow shared is halved,
and joy is doubled.
Native American saying

Close members of the same family, especially twins, often experience a higher frequency of Godwinks. The following stories exemplify ways in which guiding messages were posted along the intersecting paths of people in the same family. See if you can relate to their situations, and try to recall Godwinks that may have occurred to you with a close sibling, a parent, or a grandparent.

Twice the Godwinks

Twin sisters Susie Gray and Sandy Dahm-Schell gave birth to babies on the same day. But to Susie and Sandy, sharing their birthing experience seemed like only one more in a long line of winks that had occurred throughout their lives.

Even when they lived miles apart—one in San Diego, the other in St. Louis—they frequently picked out the same greeting cards for their parents.

The men they chose to marry are both engineers.

Six years after Sandy was married on November 7, Susie found that the only day she could book her church was November 7.

After marrying, Susie moved into her new husband's residence, only minutes away from her sister's home.

Both husbands worked at Graybar Electric in Clayton, Missouri.

When Sandy called her sister to tell her the good news that she was pregnant, Susie said, "Well, I think *I'm* pregnant too." They were surprised to learn that they both had the same due date, June 18.

On June 24—six days overdue—Susie was rushed to the hospital and gave birth. Fourteen hours later, Sandy had her baby in the room that her sister had just vacated, assisted by the same doctor.

In forty years of tracking 900 families with twins, the University of Louisville had no other record of twins giving birth to children on the same day at the same hospital.

For Susie and Sandy, their long string of Godwinks are assurances that they are going in the right direction in their lives and that they are never alone.

Holocaust survivors reunited

Two of the Hollander brothers thought they were the only family members to survive the Holocaust. The last time Alex and Ernest saw their brother Zoltan was just before the Nazis rounded up the family and shipped them to the extermination camp at Auschwitz.

For fifty years, Alex and Ernest believed that Zoltan had been killed there. "Yeah, that's what I knew—that he was hanged and he's not alive," said Ernest.

But when Ernest appeared on the *Montel Williams* television program to talk about the Holocaust, a man viewing the program thought he looked just like a tenant then living in his father's apartment building back in Yugoslavia, Zoltan Hollander. He called the show, and they researched the story. When the man's hunch proved true, Zoltan was flown to America for a tearful reunion.

For five decades, Alex, Ernest, and Zoltan were separated. But the Godwink of a stranger watching television who thought that Ernest looked like a former neighbor was the connective alignment which brought them back together again.

Bloodlines that bind

It is good to revisit Godwinks involving family members, which signaled that your future was hopeful and that you were on the right course. Following are some questions to help you probe your memory. When a Godwink comes to mind, no matter how small, jot it down in your wink diary.

1. Reconstruct the memory of a family gathering such as a wedding, a holiday, or a reunion of some sort. Who was there from the family? Picture each person, holding them in your thoughts for a few moments while you ask, "Was there something unusual that occurred with that person, either then or at another time?"

2. Who surprised you? What was the occasion? Was there a time when a brother, a sister, or a favorite aunt or uncle popped into your life with an accompanying coincidence? Did you get something totally unexpected?

3. Think of a time when you cried in the presence of family members. Who went away? Or died? Or who did something so touching that your eyes welled with tears? Was there a wink there?

4. Think of a time when a pet came into your life or suddenly left the family. Was there a Godwink associated with that incident?

5. Think of a time when you achieved something you were very proud of. Can you see a family member

smiling at you, providing support? Was there a God-wink connected to that achievement?

When you jot down even the smallest Godwinks, you will begin to stir the bottom of your memory pool, and winks from God will rise to the surface. As you continue reading this book, keep relating every story to your own history, continually combing your mind to find the confirmations that a universal power has indeed been winking at you for your lifetime, letting you know that you are on the right path.

> *Listen to your father who gave you life,*
> *and do not despise your mother when she is old.*
> —PROVERBS 23:22 NIV

10

Life-Saving Godwinks

When written in Chinese the word "crisis"
is composed of two characters.
One represents danger. The other represents opportunity.
John F. Kennedy

Imagine looking straight up at a wall of sheer rock, as far as your eye can see. Then picture yourself climbing it—without ropes or protection—just your hands and feet seeking precarious finger- and toeholds in tiny cracks as you inch your way upward. Your life depends on your own wits, strength, and presence of mind.

Now imagine voluntarily undertaking this challenge, alone, in the wilderness. This is how Seth Greenblatt reaches clarity with himself and God. "The rush for survival was something I sought whenever I found myself struggling with God," he said. "If He was really there, then He would help me overcome my fear and complete my climb."

Nothing clarifies the value of life more than having it hang in the balance.

You may not share Seth's urge to literally place yourself on the very edge of life to hear God's voice or see the wink. But I bet that you *have* stepped off a curb—thinking that traffic was clear—and found yourself nearly run over by a passing car. It's those kinds of "close calls" that give you a greater appreciation of how precious life is.

As I take you through the following stories, each involving people whose lives have hung in the balance, try to remember times when your life was placed on the edge, and fully appreciate how winks from God saved *you* from premature termination.

The heaven-sent cast call

Seth Greenblatt's rock climbing, along with his training for the Arizona State wrestling team, had put him in tiptop shape. He was having a very promising year in wrestling competitions, his studies were going well, and he should have been at peace with himself.

Yet he dropped out. The desire to emulate his brother Shon's emerging success as a film actor in Los Angeles was just too compelling. Shon's anecdotes about working on the *Nightmare on Elm Street* film series were exciting and enticing. Why not take a break, he told himself—and the others who challenged him—to study awhile in the "school of hard knocks." He and his brother could be roommates. It would be fun.

The brothers found an apartment in Hollywood's Cedars-Sinai area. They knew that, initially, they probably would not see much of each other because Shon's shooting schedule was invariably all night long.

One evening, feeling out of sorts because the move had disrupted his regular fitness routine, Seth began jumping rope in the living room.

Suddenly a piercing pain stabbed his forehead. It encircled his head. Wooziness swept over him. His knees buckled. Slumping to the floor, Seth passed out—alone in the apartment.

Across town on the set, Shon was awaiting instructions in the cast staging area. The all-night schedule had continued for several weeks without a break, and frankly, he couldn't wait for a night off.

The production manager approached the cast. "Good news, guys. We don't need you anymore tonight."

Suddenly, Shon and his colleagues were rejuvenated as they gathered their belongings and left the set. His brother would still be awake, thought Shon. It would be fun to surprise him. Instead, it was Shon who was surprised and shocked to find his brother's prone body on the floor.

Quickly, he called 911.

Within minutes, Seth was lifted into an ambulance and sped three short blocks to Cedars-Sinai Medical Center, where he was diagnosed with a critical brain aneurysm.

The good news was that Cedars-Sinai is noted for having one of the best neurological departments in the world. And the doctors said it was miraculous that Shon was able to summon help so quickly.

Seth would survive.

This time, Seth hadn't voluntarily put himself on the precipice of life. This time, he was placed there by fate.

Later, Seth recounted the combined Godwinks that saved him and provided a far greater clarity to the value of life than the sheerest cliff face ever could: First, the alteration to his brother's schedule that brought Shon home early that night, able to summon help before it was too late. Second, the Godwink that they had chosen a new apartment just a short distance from Cedars-Sinai Medical Center, which—another wink—was the best hospital in the Los Angeles area to treat a brain aneurysm.

Seth Greenblatt continued to climb sheer rock faces, placing himself on precipices. But he was grateful for the winks from God that saved his life.

Godwinks in the nick of time

Dr. Louis Graber looked at his watch, estimating what time he needed to leave the Milwaukee medical conference in order to return to Oshkosh, Wisconsin, where he was scheduled to be on duty at the hospital. He decided he ought to leave right away.

As he was walking toward the exit, a seminar poster hanging outside one of the meeting rooms caught his attention. It was a lecture for a delicate procedure—interesting perhaps, but unlikely to be used in his capacity as a surgeon at Mercy Medical Center in Oshkosh. He glanced at his watch again. If he took in the seminar, he might be late.

In Oshkosh, it was a sweltering morning. Eric Fellman, a recent college graduate, had a summer job spraying herbicide along railroad right-of-ways, driving a specially designed contraption that straddled the railroad tracks. It was a truck with a tank in the back and was fitted with rollers that could be lowered to ride the tracks while simultaneously lifting the wheels from the ground.

About to start his day, Eric was having breakfast at Bob's Big Boy a short distance from the crossing where he'd begin his tasks.

He was thinking about his fiancée, Joy. Their wedding was only eight weeks away. His thoughts drifted to her sweet voice over the motel telephone the night before and a warm, long-distance hug on a lonely evening. He smiled at the memory. "Oh, Eric, I can't wait till you're here and we're married," she had said just before hanging up.

Eric climbed into the rig parked near the restaurant. *Click.* Something was wrong with the fifteen-ton vehicle. Dismounting, Eric slid under the engine to check for a loose starter.

Suddenly the machine lurched forward. He thought he'd set the brakes! Before he could slide out to safety, a huge steel roller crushed his face and chest. Lights flashed in his mind. Warm liquid gushed into his mouth. The pain was unbearable. In an instant, Eric's life had taken a totally unexpected detour.

Normally, 95 percent of his day was spent on isolated stretches of train track between small country villages. It was therefore a miracle the accident occurred where it did—at a restaurant parking lot. Someone saw the accident and called for help.

To Eric, time moved like molasses before he felt a vague sensation of being pulled, lifted, and rolled onto a gurney. He heard the slamming of ambulance doors and the muffled sound of a siren. Emergency-room doctors made a hurried, ominous assessment of Eric's condition. His midsection was badly crushed. He was losing large quantities of blood. All of his vital signs had plunged. They feared the worst: rupture of the liver.

The liver acts like a sponge, and it cannot be simply stitched closed. Survival from a burst liver was doubtful. As Eric entered surgery, the worst thing *did* happen. His liver ruptured.

But then, God winked.

Dr. Louis Graber entered the operating room. Just back

from attending the seminar in Milwaukee, he assessed the situation. He couldn't believe it.

He *had* taken in that last lecture. It revealed a new technique to mend a ruptured liver. Now, that very technique was what the situation called for. While the liver itself could not be sutured, Dr. Graber, remembering the seminar, skillfully drew membrane from the surrounding area, folded and clamped it, and the bleeding stopped.

Hours later, Eric opened his eyes to see Joy's loving eyes smiling back at him.

The wedding date needed to be changed, allowing for rehabilitation, but weeks later when Eric Fellman finally was able to stand at his wedding before his family and friends, he said, "A wedding is a celebration. And this one is doubly festive. We are celebrating both the miracle of God saving my life and the miracle of God giving me Joy."

The Godwink of Dr. Graber squeezing in that last lecture at the conference and still leaving in time to save the life of Eric Fellman was surely a magnificent divinely aligned wink from God.

A penny saved . . .

Sammy was two years old and unable to explain what had happened to him. He looked fragile. His breathing was labored. "That child had an angelic face," Dr. Lester Coleman said later, "the kind of little kid you just wanted to pick up and hug."

Sammy's distressed mother said that he had been playing with pennies, and she thought he might have swallowed one.

Soon, Dr. Coleman and an x-ray technician were hunched over a transparency of Sammy's chest. There, in clear view, was a penny lodged in the boy's windpipe. Dr. Coleman promptly called for surgery. If the coin was not removed, the child would choke to death.

Dr. Coleman conferred with his medical team. The anesthesiologist voiced a fear that if the child was anesthetized by insertion of a bronchoscope into his larynx and trachea, the instrument itself would cause swelling. That would result in the walls of the larynx and trachea pressing against each other, further tightening their grip on the coin. What could they do?

Dr. Coleman pondered for a moment and then provided the strategy: If the anesthesiologist could bring Sammy's breathing down to the lowest level—still within the parameters of safety—for a mere fifteen seconds, he believed that he could enter the relaxed organ and retrieve the obstacle.

The operating room crackled with efficiency. On cue from the anesthesiologist, Dr. Coleman nodded to his team. In a synchronized, rehearsed motion, a nurse handed him a metal tube, which was inserted into the boy's mouth and throat. She slapped forceps into his palm, which were inserted into the metal tube, and just as quickly, the forceps reappeared, gripping the troublesome penny.

It all happened within fifteen seconds—prompting spontaneous applause in the operating room.

The following morning, Dr. Coleman was entering surgery with another patient when a nurse advised him that Sammy and his mother were about to be released from the hospital. Dr. Coleman felt an inexplicable urge to personally say good-bye and hug Sammy before he left.

"Tell you what," he whispered conspiratorially to the nurse. "Stall them for me, will you? Tell 'em you need another set of x-rays before they can go—that way, I can get one more hug from that sweet little kid."

Never before had he ordered a second set of x-rays, and he felt a little guilty that his desire for a hug would create an additional cost. A short while later, Dr. Coleman briskly exited the operating room, en route to bid farewell to his little patient. Passing the x-ray department, he noted the technician staring at an x-ray with a puzzled expression.

"Why are you looking at Sammy's old x-ray?" asked Dr. Coleman, noticing the clear image of a penny in the child's larynx and trachea.

"I'm not. This is the *new* x-ray."

"What?" said Dr. Coleman, gaping in astonishment.

Sammy had swallowed not one but *two* pennies. The two coins were neatly stacked, one exactly behind the other, giving the appearance on the first x-ray of only one penny.

Once more, Sammy was rushed into the operating room, where Dr. Coleman, his anesthesiologist, and the operating team repeated the fifteen-second extraction procedure of the day before.

A short while later, Sammy was resting comfortably. Had he returned home, he most likely would have died. But a marvelous, mysterious force intervened with a life-altering Godwink, prompting Dr. Coleman to take one more x-ray just so he could obtain one more hug.

You will never convince Dr. Lester Coleman that these events were caused merely by chance. "God always *was* my surgical assistant," he said.

Thank your fortuitous winks

The Godwinks that you may have experienced—such as that time you nearly stepped off a curb into the path of a speeding car—might not have been as dramatic as those told here; nonetheless, the outcome for you was just as decisive: your life was saved by a fortuitous intervening action in a blink of time. You may not have even been aware that your life was close to the edge.

Looking back on the preceding stories, you will see that it was the perfection of God's timing that interceded at the crucial moment to save a life. My grandmother would say, "God's timing is not your timing, my son, but he's never late."

> *It is not for you to know the times or dates*
> *the Father has set by his own authority.*
>
> —ACTS 1:7 NIV

11

Godwinks at Life's End

Death and love are two wings
that bear the good man to heaven.
M. Angelo

Godwinks are seldom more prevalent than at the end of life. Yet winks from God are not communications to those who die; they are messages of hope to the living, providing reassurance that the person who died has a role to play in the infinite plan and that those of us who are left have a continued role here on earth.

The following stories share a thread: Every one the people left behind found comfort in either the perfect circularity of life and death or in unexpected Godwinks that could only be interpreted as friendly reassurance from another dimension.

Going out with a flourish

On Sunday, February 13, 2000, fans of Charlie Brown learned that Charles Schulz, creator of their beloved *Pea-

nuts comic strip, had died in his sleep of a heart attack. The timing of his death was jolting: After a run of almost fifty years in newspapers in seventy-five countries, he died just as the final Sunday *Peanuts* strip was going to press. Schulz had announced three months earlier that the comic strip would end its run because he was suffering from colon cancer.

His good-bye for the last *Peanuts* funny page proved to be his epitaph. Here's what he wrote:

> *Dear Friends,*
>
> *I have been fortunate to draw Charlie Brown and his friends for almost 50 years. It has been the fulfillment of my childhood ambition.*
>
> *Unfortunately, I am no longer able to maintain the schedule demanded by a daily comic strip, therefore I am announcing my retirement.*
>
> *I have been grateful over the years for the loyalty of our editors and the wonderful support and love expressed to me by fans of the comic strip.*
>
> *Charlie Brown, Snoopy, Linus, Lucy . . . how can I ever forget them . . .*
>
> *Charles Schulz*

The most fitting tributes for him came from colleagues in the cartoon world: *Hagar the Horrible*'s Chris Brown said,

"He used the strip as therapy . . . reaching into the muck of his own soul and coming up with diamonds." *For Better or For Worse's* creator Lynn Johnston expressed the irony on most of our minds: "He made one last deadline. There's romance in that."

It is interesting to note that Charles Schulz was extremely committed to his work; he followed his own destiny. As he himself said, cartooning was his childhood ambition. To fulfill it, he used his talents to their fullest. When he reached road's end, the rightfulness of his life's work didn't stop there: His death provided a message to the living that a life well lived leads to a perfect synchronicity, even in death. The following stories further bear this out.

The golden girl

The possibility that Godwinks occur with greater frequency at the end of one's life occurred to me following the death of NBC anchorwoman Jessica Savitch. I first became aware of her when I was in charge of ABC's *Good Morning America* program. I was looking for David Hartman's new co-host. The first candidates that came to mind were Joan Lunden, who anchored local news on New York's WABC-TV, and Jessica Savitch, whose charming yet authoritative on-camera persona on NBC had impressed me.

Lunden became the top choice when Savitch's agent advised me that her contractual commitments were ironclad, making her availability out of the question. I dropped any attempt to even meet with her.

Three years later, Jessica Savitch was killed in a freak accident near New Hope, Pennsylvania. Blinded by dense fog as her car backed away from a restaurant parking lot adjacent to the Delaware River canal, Jessica and a friend drowned when they plunged twelve feet to the canal below.

I happened to be vacationing in New Hope four weeks after the accident and was overcome by a deep melancholy and regret when a waiter informed me that I was dining at the same restaurant where the tragedy had occurred. It was a sadness that she had died so young. I felt a regret that I had so easily given up my pursuit to meet her to tell her how much I had admired her work.

"Coincidentally," on my first day back in the office after that vacation, I received a letter from a woman named Alanna Nash, who said she was writing a biography on Jessica, and she wished to interview me.

Me, of all people. I promptly replied that while I had held Jessica Savitch in the highest esteem, I, unfortunately, could be of no use in compiling her biography, as we'd never met.

A week or so later, another letter from Alanna Nash was lying on my desk. "You must be mistaken," she wrote. "You *must* have known Jessica, for she wrote about *you* in her autobiography."

What? My mind raced in bewilderment. Lying next to the letter was a book. I vaguely remembered my secretary, Elaine Alestra, saying there was something I should read— something about a book she just happened to have. It was Jessica Savitch's autobiography, and a bookmark poked from the pages.

The words caused my eyes to moisten as my mind struggled to remember a job interview with a young woman years before at WBZ in Boston. Here is Jessica Savitch's memory of that occasion, in her own words:

I sent letters . . . and finally got a casual reply from WBZ in Boston. If anyone even intimated he would see me—"If ever in your travels you find yourself in the area, give us a call."—I would be there the next day. Jeff Greenhart, a classmate . . . who was living on Beacon Hill . . . made time to meet me at the Greyhound bus station and drive me to the interview.

SQuire Rushnell, head of ABC programming, interviewed me: "This is a tough business to break into," he began (that was always the first statement I heard). He didn't hire me, but he spent about an hour with me that afternoon, showing me around the news set. Afterwards I took a cab over to Jeff's.

"How'd it go?" he asked.

"Really well."

"Did you get the job?"

"No."

"Then how could it have gone well?"

"I think he took me seriously."

The time he gave me was my first hint of encouragement.

So many thoughts crossed my mind. Why had I visited the very restaurant where Jessica Savitch died? How strange that the letter from Alanna Nash would arrive just after my return from vacation and that my secretary would just happen to have the autobiography in which Jessica implied that her meeting with me was a small milestone in her life.

The next chapter to the story unfolded during a meeting with Judy Girard, head of programming for the Lifetime Television Channel. After congratulating her on Lifetime's television movie *Golden Girl: The Jessica Savitch Story*, the season's highest-rated film, I told her about my Jessica Savitch experience. To my surprise, she described her own Godwinks with Jessica Savitch, beginning with the fact that she and Jessica were roommates at the University of Pennsylvania.

The Savitch movie had been proposed to Judy by a Los Angeles producer, who did not know that she and Jessica had been friends. Judy's initial reaction was negative: She knew some pretty confidential things about her former roommate, and there was no way a movie could be made truthfully without hurting Jessica's family.

But another Godwink a few weeks later altered her thinking. Judy had a speaking engagement before the Jessica Savitch Scholarship graduates at the University of Pennsylvania. She was pleased to find that Jessica's sisters were there, providing her with the unexpected opportunity to broach the idea of a film. Not only were the sisters supportive, but they agreed to oversee production of a post-film documentary on the real Jessica Savitch.

Just as unusual as my experience—finding out after her death that I had not only known Jessica Savitch but had actually touched her life in a small way—was Judy Girard's Godwink. She knew Jessica well, yet she could never have anticipated that a movie pitch from a producer—who had no idea that she and Jessica had been roommates—would come just before a "chance" meeting with her sisters, thereby delivering her, and Lifetime, the opportunity to develop their highest-rated movie.

Barbra Streisand's wink from the grave

The 1983 movie *Yentl* was about a young Jewish girl who achieved her wish to study the Torah, a practice once available only to males, by disguising herself as a young man. Barbra Streisand not only starred in it and directed it, but she also wrote it.

"I was particularly committed to the film," she said, "because, in a way, it was a tribute to my father, who died when I was a young child."

The film's connection to her father was evident—the first words uttered on the screen are, "Yentl, how's Papa?" And when the father dies, Barbra sings, "Papa, can you help me not to be frightened? . . . I remember everything you taught me. . . . Papa, how I miss you kissing me good night."

After the script was finished, Barbra felt compelled to do something she'd never done before: she went to her father's grave. As she quietly absorbed the peace and serenity of the cemetery, she wished there was a way for her father to know that this film was in his honor.

Lost in thought and memories, her eyes were drawn to the grave beside her father's. The name on the grave marker provided a startling Godwink—and a jolting confirmation. "Written on the gravestone," said Barbra, "was the name of the boy that I had come up with in the script for the star of my film."

It was an unusual Yiddish name: Anshel.

"What a 'coincidence,' huh?" said Streisand.

Mother's winks of comfort

Carolyn Schroth was devastated. A freak mid-April snowstorm had caused her mother's car to skid out of control, killing her instantly. Her mother was her best friend. People remarked that they were like schoolgirls together, commuting side by side on weekdays, and golfing or skiing together on weekends.

Carolyn's mom was a talented and successful New York fashion illustrator for newspaper ads, selling her services to agencies that represented department stores. Subsequent to college, her mom encouraged Carolyn to accept a job with an ad agency and to be "brave enough to take the train into New York City every day."

But after her mother's death, Carolyn felt empty nearly every moment of every day. The daily walk from work to Grand Central Station was lonely without her mother. One evening at dusk, Carolyn walked along the street across from the office building in which her mother's first client was located. The building had a brightly lit storefront window. Something in the window caught Carolyn's eye.

It was her mother! Her mother was sitting in the window!

Quickly crossing the street, Carolyn's heart raced. Her head swam with bewilderment. Staring into the window, Carolyn realized that it was a mannequin—in her mother's exact image, dressed like her, leaning over a drawing table covered with fashion pictures and magazines. The mannequin was looking at an open calendar that referenced a skiing date. Also written on the calendar were these words: "Lunch with Tommy" and "Call Ray."

Tommy was Carolyn's younger brother. Ray was her father.

The lifeless form was eerie and riveting. "It was like a ghost," Carolyn said. Over the next few weeks, Carolyn stopped in front of the window every day to stare at the image of her mother. Each time she felt a little better. Each time she sensed a secret connection with her mom, steering her toward the belief that her mother was in another place that was good.

"I believe there was something behind all those things that happened. Something to do with eternal life—a connection with the supernatural. The Godwinks reaffirmed that my mother was subtly helping me," said Carolyn.

A short while after this story was written, I was asked to give a talk from the pulpit at my church, Quaker Hill Church in Pawling, New York. Upon my arrival, the deacon handed me a list of thirteen names. It was customary, after the talk and before the final hymn, for the speaker to conduct a prayer of concern for various members of the congregation.

During my talk I had told the Carolyn Schroth story knowing that while she now lived in San Francisco, she had grown up in the Quaker Hill area, and some people might remember her. The congregation was visibly taken with my comments and was particularly moved by Carolyn's experience.

Afterwards, I led the prayer for those on the concerns list, slowly articulating the name of each person. The last name on the list stopped me cold. My eyes moistened as I shared with the congregation the Godwink that had just been delivered to all of us: The last name on the list for whom our prayers were directed was Ray Schroth—Carolyn's father.

Kermit the Frog and his composer

Jim Henson, the genius who created the Muppets, was deeply connected to Joe Raposo, the man who composed most of the hit songs for *Sesame Street*, the innovative program for children.

Among the many ways the two men were closely identified was Kermit the Frog's signature melody *It Isn't Easy Being Green*, which spoke quietly of racial discrimination. Henson was the voice of Kermit, and Raposo wrote the song. Henson and Raposo shared something else: they both died young. On February 5, 1989, Raposo died at the age of fifty-one. His life and music was celebrated in a television special called *Sing* on the Public Broadcasting System, May 16, 1990.

May 16, 1990 was the very day that Henson died—at age fifty-three.

Godwinks are messages to the living

At times when you are deeply grieving, you may not understand *why* a loved one was called to the other side. But Godwinks are loving messages of hope meant to reassure you that life is not a continuum but a circle, and that connections to loved ones are never lost.

In the preceding stories, these winks were for the benefit of the living:

- In the Jessica Savitch story, the Godwink received by Judy Girard when she encountered Jessica's sisters, as she considered whether to produce a biographical drama about Jessica, reassured her that the movie should be made.
- Barbra Streisand received a wink, literally from the grave, while making a movie dedicated to her father that helped her to come to terms with his death.
- Carolyn Schroth was comforted by the mannequin in the store window that looked like her mother, and she took its presence as a sign that her mother was in a better place.
- Jim Henson's family and friends struggled to make sense of his early death. But the television special about his collaborator being broadcast on the very day of Henson's death was a wink from God to them,

and they took comfort from it as evidence that there is divine order to this world.

When someone you admire or someone close to you dies, hold tightly to this truth: Everything *will* be OK. You are seeing but one small piece of the overall puzzle. From God's perspective, it all makes perfect sense.

The Lord is close to the brokenhearted
and saves those who are crushed in spirit.
—PSALM 34:18 NIV

12

Godwinks in History

*Be enthusiastic. Determine to succeed.
And love your country.*
Carlos J. Arboleya

The two men who were most involved in the writing of the Declaration of Independence, John Adams and Thomas Jefferson, both died on exactly the same day in 1826.

The same day! But it wasn't just *any* day. They died on the Fourth of July, the date on which that historic document was signed! But it wasn't just *any* Fourth of July. It was the fiftieth anniversary of the signing of the Declaration of Independence.

As I sat in my small study, pondering these Godwinks, I wondered whether there were more divinely aligned "coincidences" connecting the two men during their lives. To find an answer, I decided to research the date of their death. Perhaps whoever was president of the United States in July 1826 had delivered a eulogy or had remarked about the "coincidence" of their dying on the same day.

I crossed the room and pulled a reference book from the

shelf of my modest library collection. I learned that the man who occupied the White House at the time of Adams's and Jefferson's deaths was John Quincy Adams, the son of John Adams. *That's interesting*, I thought. But the book was devoid of any reference to a eulogy or any remarks at all by John Quincy Adams on the "coincidental" date of the two men's deaths.

My eye was then drawn to a thin black volume right next to the book I'd pulled off the shelf. I had never opened it in the twelve years since I'd returned from my grandfather's funeral with a box of books. No wonder I had ignored the homely little book. Its title was totally uninviting: *Webster's Great Orations*.

Inside, the title page offered little more enticement. An ancient typeface proclaimed *The Great Orations and Senatorial Speeches of Daniel Webster*. But imagine my amazement to see that the first of Webster's speeches, delivered on August 2, 1826, was titled "The Eulogy for Adams and Jefferson."

It was exactly what I was looking for! As I read, Senator Webster's elegant prose leapt from the pages as it described an extraordinary number of other "coincidences" between these two heroes of history. Here, in Daniel Webster's own eloquent words, is a portion of the eulogy:

> Adams and Jefferson are now no more. But the concurrence of their death, with such coincidence,

on the anniversary of Independence, has naturally awakened strong emotions.

It cannot but seem striking and extraordinary that these two should live to see the fiftieth year from the date of that act; that they should complete that year; and that, on the day which had fast linked forever their own fame with their country's glory, the heavens should open to receive them both at once.

There were many points of similarity in the lives and fortunes of Adams and Jefferson. They both were learned and able lawyers. They were natives and inhabitants, respectively, of those two of the colonies, which at the revolution, were the largest and most powerful, and which naturally had a lead in the political affairs of the times.

Both were not only decided but early friends of Independence. While others yet doubted, they were resolved; where others hesitated, they pressed forward.

They were both members of the committee for preparing the Declaration of Independence, and they constituted the sub-committee, appointed by the other members, to make the draught.

Both have been public ministers abroad, both vice presidents, and both presidents.

These coincidences are now singularly crowned and completed. They have died, together, and they died on the anniversary of liberty.

May not such events raise the suggestion that they are not undesigned, and that Heaven does so order things, as sometimes to attract strongly the attention, and excite the thoughts of men?

My sentiments exactly! I glanced at the publication date of the book: 1853. Another question flashed through my mind. Imagine if I had, in my research, learned that the very eulogy on Adams and Jefferson that I was seeking was contained in a little book called *Webster's Great Orations*, published nearly one and a half centuries before. Would it be possible to find that book today?

For the fun of it, I checked the computer of every public library in the East. There was no evidence of the book's existence. I felt disappointment, a lack of validation—until I later found a single copy of the book, in the rare book section of the Library of Congress. As far as I know, there exists only two copies of *Webster's Great Orations*. The one in the nation's library and the one passed down to me from my grandfather which had been sitting right there on a nearby shelf waiting for me to find it and read it. What are the odds of that?

God winked big time!

Lincoln–Kennedy parallels

Perhaps you have heard about the astonishing parallels between two other presidents: Abraham Lincoln and John F. Kennedy. Consider these uncanny "coincidences" that are listed at the Ford Theater, the place of Lincoln's assassination, in Washington, D.C.:

- Both Lincoln and Kennedy were elected to the presidency exactly one hundred years apart, in 1860 and 1960.
- Both Lincoln and Kennedy each had to bury a child who had died during their occupancy of the White House.
- President Lincoln's secretary was named Kennedy. President Kennedy's secretary was named Lincoln.
- Each of their secretaries advised them not to go to the places where they were assassinated: Lincoln to the theater, Kennedy to Dallas, Texas.
- Both were assassinated in the presence of their wives by gunshot wounds to the back of the head.
- The vice presidents who succeeded the assassinated presidents were both former senators, both from the South, and both named Johnson.
- Both vice presidents, Andrew Johnson and Lyndon Johnson, were born exactly one hundred years apart, in 1808 and 1908.

- Both assassins had three names totaling fifteen letters: John Wilkes Booth and Lee Harvey Oswald.
- Both assassins were born one hundred years apart, in 1839 and 1939.
- Booth shot Lincoln in a theater and ran to a warehouse. Oswald shot Kennedy from his perch in a warehouse and ran to a theater.
- Both assassins were killed before they were brought to trial.
- Lincoln and Kennedy both left a legacy for the advancement of civil rights.
- Both presidents' last names contain seven letters.

John F. Kennedy–George W. Bush parallels

On November 17, 2000, the *Washington Post* reported another list of startling presidential parallels comparing the 1960 election between John F. Kennedy and Richard Nixon and the 2000 election between George W. Bush and Al Gore.

- Both the 1960 and 2000 elections were the closest in American history.
- Both presidential candidates who were sitting vice presidents—Nixon and Gore—were smart, politically savvy, and a bit stiff on the campaign trail.

- Both of their opponents—Kennedy and Bush—were rich and handsome with a reputation for youthful misbehavior.
- The television networks prematurely called both elections only to change their predictions later.
- Each vice president—Nixon and Gore—issued a partial concession and then recanted it.
- Both the Nixon and Gore campaigns complained of voter irregularities and called for recounts.
- In both elections, members of the powerful Daley family from Chicago played an integral role. In 1960, Chicago Mayor Richard Daley was accused of misusing his political machine to tilt the Illinois victory to the Democrats. His son, former Secretary of Commerce William Daley, was Democrat Al Gore's campaign manager.
- In both elections the vice presidents—Nixon and Gore—lost.

While it is fascinating to reflect on the Godwinks that have occurred in history, it's even more interesting to see them in your own life. Just as with famous historical figures, the Godwinks in your life have formed a chain of winks. And like the lines painted along the highways, your Godwinks have quietly helped you to stay on course throughout life.

Still, Godwinks are not subtle; they jolt us, awaken us to the marvelous possibilities that God's ordered world provides for us. To paraphrase Daniel Webster, "coincidences" excite our thoughts and open our minds to our own potential to fulfill our role, our destiny, in the world. (I cannot fault Senator Webster for not using the word "Godwink." It wasn't invented yet.)

> *Therefore encourage one another and*
> *build one another up, just as you are doing.*
> —1 THESSALONIANS 5:11 ESV

13

Godwinks in the Arts

*You have to leave room for God
to walk through the room.*
Quincy Jones

People in the arts, because of their natural creativity, are perhaps more likely to see Godwinks as signs of hope and encouragement meant just for them. Supporting that point, following are stories involving artists, authors, and actors.

A tale of two Reeves

One man was named Reeves. The other was named Reeve. Both grew up to be actors. Both were cast as Superman. Both had career downturns. Both suffered great tragedy.

In the 1950s, George Reeves landed the lead in television's *The Adventures of Superman* series and enjoyed great popularity for seven seasons. But typecasting as Superman made it difficult to find work when the series ended. He even considered becoming a professional wrestler. In 1959, misfortune struck. George Reeves was found dead of a gunshot wound to the head—ruled a suicide but believed by some to be murder.

In 1978, Christopher Reeve landed the lead in a *Superman* motion picture and enjoyed popularity through four sequels. But typecasting also limited the roles he subsequently was able to command, sending him into smaller movie roles and summer theater productions. In 1995, he also met misfortune. A fall from a horse left him a quadriplegic—paralyzed from the neck down.

Ironically, Christopher Reeve's last film before his equestrian accident was *Above Suspicion*; he played a paralyzed policeman. That film was still in the theaters when Reeve, thrown from a horse, became paralyzed himself.

Why George Reeves and Christopher Reeve were on such parallel paths is a mystery—a puzzle piece whose role in the larger picture is still today difficult to understand. When I discussed the remarkable chain of "coincidences" with television producer Gary Grossman—himself a Superman movie buff—he had a Superman "coincidence" story of his own.

Gary was writing a book called *Superman: Serial to Cereal* in 1976. He had completed interviews with all of the key people who had worked on the *Superman* television series except for one: Noel Neill, one of the two women who had played Lois Lane. On his way to meet her, Gary was apprehensive. Would she be cooperative?

Hoping to break the ice, Gary pulled over at a T-shirt shop on Hollywood Boulevard to buy Ms. Neill a small gift: a classic Superman T-shirt. Emerging from the shop, Gary was startled by the sound of screeching tires and blaring horns. His package slipped out of his arms and fell to the sidewalk.

"I reached down to pick it up and I froze, staring at where the bag had landed. It had fallen atop a sidewalk star on the Hollywood Walk of Fame—the *very* star belonging to Superman George Reeves. I didn't even know that George Reeves *had* a star on Hollywood Boulevard," said Gary, "but to this day, I somehow feel I met him in that single moment."

Regarding that exceptional Godwink, Gary concluded, "I like to think that someone was saying, 'Hello, Gary. Good luck with the book.'"

The cartoonist and his hero

Mike Peters won the Pulitzer Prize for his *Mother Goose & Grimm* comic strip. His unique style was developed during his teen years through a steady diet of cartoon art by his hero, Bill Mauldin, the illustrator famous for drawing World War II foot soldiers. Their eventual meeting inaugurated a lifelong friendship, and it was Mauldin who recommended Peters to the *Daily News* in Dayton, Ohio, where Peters's career flourished.

And it was through a Godwink that Bill Mauldin un-knowingly connected again to Mike Peters and his wife, Marian, on the biggest move of their lives—*away* from Dayton. "Dayton was a wonderful place to live," says Mike. "We raised our three children there, and the *Daily News* was a terrific home base for my syndicated comic strip and daily editorial cartoons."

"We had never even considered leaving," added Marian. But a 1990 job offer in Atlanta raised the possibility of living in a less wintry locale. Although Mike turned down the offer, he confessed to his editor in Dayton that the seduction had caused him and Marian to ask, "Why not consider doing my work in a warmer climate?"

The editor concurred that a long-distance working relationship was certainly feasible. A few days later, Mike was preparing to leave for a long-planned trip to a classic-cartoon festival in Sarasota, Florida. In a passing conversation with his neighbor, a real-estate broker, he shared the story of his boss's willingness to set up a long-distance working arrangement. The neighbor suggested to Mike and Marian that they ought to put their house on the market while they were away, "just to sample the marketplace."

"Sure, why not?" shrugged Mike. But just as they were leaving for Florida, Mike and Marian were greeted with a surprise: their neighbor already had a firm offer for their home. Would they accept it?

Suddenly facing a crossroads, they pondered the question all the way to Florida. While there, they decided to take a look at one or two homes for sale, just to get a feel for the real-estate market there.

"This house is on a lovely little pond," noted the broker as the front door of the first home was opened to greet them.

"Marian! Hi!"

What a Godwink! The owner was Sandy Strom, one of Marian's former sorority sisters from Dayton. They'd lost touch twenty years earlier. That wink helped convince Mike and Marian that they were indeed on the right path—that a move from Dayton was going to be just fine.

And the Godwinks didn't stop there.

Mike and Marian learned that the "lovely little pond" did not belong to them. It was owned by a neighbor. Their concerns rose as they considered what might happen if the pond were ever sold. At a neighborhood welcoming party, Mike and Marian met the man who owned it. They asked him if he would consider selling it.

"Sorry," said the man. "Others have been interested, but I'm not inclined to sell." Mike and Marian's hearts fell.

"What do you do?" the man asked Mike. When Mike explained that he was a cartoonist, the man exclaimed, "Say, you must know Bill Mauldin."

Mike literally jumped in enthusiasm. "Of course, I

know him. He's my lifelong mentor. In fact, just last week, Marian and I visited Bill at his home in Palm Springs, California."

"In Palm Springs!" said the neighbor, amazed. "That's *my* house! I rented my Palm Springs house to Bill Mauldin."

The extraordinary power of those winks from God struck the neighbor as an unmistakable sign that he should reconsider his decision, and so he *did* sell Mike and Marian the pond. And, because of all the signs directing them to Florida, Mike and Marian Peters have always felt somewhat charmed by their home in Sarasota.

There are times in your life when you—like Mike and Marian Peters—are faced with tough decisions; you feel as though you are standing at a fork in the road. Should you go this way or that way? These are the times when you need to begin looking for Godwinks as reassurances that you are indeed choosing the right path. When you see them, get on the path, knowing you can move forward with the confidence that you are being divinely aligned.

The Titanic sinks twice

The movie *Titanic* was the highest-grossing film of all time, underscoring the universal power and durability of the tragic story. In real life, of course, the *Titanic* was a magnificently built trans-Atlantic passenger ship, thought to be unsinkable, but it collided with an iceberg and sank on its first voyage from Southampton, England, in April 1912. Nearly 1,500 people, or two-thirds of the 2,224 passengers, froze to death or drowned in the icy Atlantic Ocean because the ship held an insufficient number of lifeboats.

And here's the "coincidence": Fourteen years before the *Titanic* took its fateful voyage, Morgan Robertson wrote a fictional story called *Futility; or, The Wreck of the Titan*. Here are some of the details, which parallel the fictitious ship the *Titan* versus the real *Titanic*:

- Both departed from Southampton, England.
- Both were supposedly unsinkable.
- Both struck an iceberg on the starboard side, near midnight.
- In both cases, the tragedy occurred in the month of April.
- Both lacked sufficient lifeboats.
- Both sent most of their passengers and crew to their frigid deaths in the North Atlantic.

How did Mr. Robertson know? Was it his highly developed creative sensibilities that allowed him to tune in to events that had not yet occurred? Was the book's publication meant as a warning, a Godwink, sadly ignored, by those whose hubris and pride later contributed to the tragedy?

Sadly, those who should have noticed the Godwink didn't see it.

Where the Twain shall meet

Mark Twain had searched high and low trying to find a copy of the magazine containing an article he'd written years earlier. He wrote to the publisher, asking for a duplicate.

"Sorry," they replied. "The demand was so enormous for your article that we are unable to locate a single copy."

A few weeks later, Twain was in New York City, waiting for a traffic light at the corner of Fifth Avenue and 42nd Street, when a stranger in the crowd recognized him. "Mr. Twain!" said the man. "I was just on my way to the post office to mail you this package. Last night I was cleaning out some old files and found something I thought you might like. Here—you saved me some postage."

Puzzled, Twain watched the man disappear into the crowd. Slowly he opened the envelope and stood on the busy street for several seconds, staring at its contents. Inside was the very magazine he had been searching for.

Mark Twain had put his wish "out there" into the ether, so to speak, and the answer came back—in a Godwink.

Creativity and Godwinks

Scientists know that right-brain-oriented people—those whose dominant hemisphere is the one controlling intuition—are more likely to be creative than those who are left-brain-oriented. Neurologist Arthur Winter, M.D., wrote of this distinction in his book *Brain Workout*, co-authored with his wife, Ruth:

> There is evidence that, in most of us, the right hemisphere of our brains is the font of creativity while the left is more logical. The left side is concerned with the spoken language, numbers, reading and reasoning. The right side . . . is involved in music awareness, three-dimensional forms, and art awareness. Imagination, intuition, and creativity are right brain activities.

Perhaps artistic people are more Godwink-conscious than others. Writers, actors, musicians, and inventors may simply be more *attuned* to matters of inspiration and more likely to actually *notice* the signs along their universal highways through life. If that's the case, how then can you develop your right brain and become more creative?

How to increase your creativity

Just as Godwinks occur to everyone, Dr. Winter believes creativity can be enhanced in just about everyone. A variety of techniques suggested by him and his wife form the basis for the following list I have devised to help enhance the creative process. Use these techniques to heighten your creativity and raise your awareness to the Godwinks happening to you.

Over the next two weeks, try employing these techniques on a specific creative endeavor—writing, drawing, finding a creative solution to a business challenge—and see if you begin to feel more creative as well as more attuned to the forces of coincidences in the universe:

- *Prepare yourself*. Read as much as you can about your endeavor and talk about whatever it is you wish to create.
- *Incubate*. We all want quick solutions, but when the answer doesn't come right away, put the thought aside. Let it simmer in your subconscious. At a later point, perhaps days later, there will be a breakthrough.
- *Test*. Once you've come up with a creative solution, try it out. New ideas need to be proved.
- *Distance yourself*. Let go of the creative endeavor for a while—walk into another room, take a "mental excursion" to a vacation you have taken, or do something else that gets your mind off the creative activity.
- *Add variety to your life*. Meet new people. Read new books. Increase the mental stimuli in your environ-

ment, inviting new thoughts and concepts to come into your thought process.

- *Don't be afraid to be alone*. You also need time to listen to your inner self instead of someone else suggesting how you should think.
- *Be disciplined*. It may seem paradoxical, but unstructured environments are not conducive to free thinking. The creative process is enhanced when you develop a structure to your plan to regularly write, paint, or otherwise develop the object of your creativity.
- *Find your best time*. There is a time of day or night when you get your best ideas. Nurture that time.
- *Find the best place*. Think about where you get your best ideas: walking on the beach, working in the garden, or cloistered in a small room. Somewhere there is a place where your creativity will be enhanced by systematically going there.
- *Keep a pen and paper handy*. Capture fleeting ideas that may later prove to be invaluable by keeping a pad and pen by the bed and in your purse or pocket. "The dullest pencil is better than the sharpest mind," my secretary Elaine Alestra often reminded me.
- *Text yourself a message*. When a great idea occurs to you and you don't have a pen and paper, text or email yourself a message. I have a composer friend who uses this technique whenever he comes up with

a new melody while driving his car or away from home; he sings or hums himself a voice mail.

- *Farm your brain.* Verbalize or write down as many ideas as you can dig out of your brain. Let your mind wander and consider all sorts of solutions.
- *Defer judgment.* Listen carefully to your own thoughts. Don't self-edit your ideas right away, saying "That's dumb" or "That won't work." Keep even the craziest ideas in circulation, and eventually quantity will produce quality.
- *Don't be afraid to make mistakes.* Creativity comes from the freedom to be willing to color outside the lines once in a while.
- *Don't make excuses.* There is no excuse for lacking creative thought—not your age, not your health, not your lot in life. For every excuse you come up with as to why you can't be creative, I bet I can come up with dozens of people in the same situation—or worse—who *can* be creative.

If you begin today to enhance your right-brain activity by elevating your creative capability—getting your mind involved in everything from creative problem-solving to trying your hand at drawing a picture—you'll be developing the part of the brain that uses intuition and imagination.

Before long, Godwinks will begin to be much more apparent to you. The more you tune in to the winks from God in your everyday life, the more you will see them.

Since we have gifts that differ
according to the grace given to us,
each of us is to exercise them accordingly.

—ROMANS 12:6 NASB

14

Godwinks in Sports

Don't follow the crowd.
Be yourself. Believe in something.
Tom Landry

It is clear that Godwinks happen to everyone. They happen to presidents of countries and to presidents of companies. They happen to celebrities and to everyday people. They happen to you and to me. God winks at everyone, in every line of work. That includes those who work or play in the world of sports.

As you read the following four sports-related stories, see if you can recall a sports Godwink that touched your life and sent you a message of encouragement.

Perfect baseball

A perfect baseball game is a highly unusual phenomenon. Apart from the flawless performance it requires from the pitcher, every one of his eight teammates must also have a perfect day fielding the ball. A game in which there are no hits, no walks, no runs, and no errors against the winning pitcher is so rare that as of July 1999 there had been only sixteen perfect baseball games in the history of American baseball.

Three of them belonged to the New York Yankees and occurred over the span of forty years. The mind-boggling Godwink is that one man, Don Larsen, was connected to all three.

Larsen was the first Yankee to pitch a perfect game. He wrote his name in the history books in the fifth game of the 1956 World Series against the Brooklyn Dodgers. Larsen's catcher that day was Yogi Berra, who said, "Next to getting in the Hall of Fame, that perfect game was probably my greatest thrill in baseball."

It took forty-two years before the Yankees had another perfect game. This time it was David Wells's turn, on May 17, 1998, against the Minnesota Twins. This game is significant to me because my son, Grant, and I were there. Someone had give.n us tickets, and they turned out to be great seats, eight rows from home plate. But until later, I had no idea how *really* great a gift those tickets were.

In the seventh inning, it dawned on us fans that something special was happening. You could almost sense a tentativeness in the crowd. In later innings as Wells came off the mound and retired to the side in the Yankee dugout, nobody talked to him.

His teammates seemed to rudely ignore their pitcher instead of congratulating him for doing such a great job. They weren't being rude. They were afraid to talk to him or to do anything to break the spell. When, in the ninth inning, Wells faced his twenty-seventh batter, and captured his final out with a fly ball to Paul O'Neill, the stadium erupted. Finally, his teammates charged the field and swarmed over him.

Dazed by such an extraordinary event, the fans lingered, some standing, others sitting, soaking in the uniqueness of the moment. Reverently, the crowd kept watching as the players filed back through the dugout toward the locker room.

David Wells's pal, pitcher David Cone, was the last man in the dugout. Noting the lingering crowd, Cone suggested that Wells take a last bow. It was the right gesture. The stadium erupted once more as the man of the hour took off his cap and waved to his fans.

How was Don Larsen, the first perfect-game Yankee connected to Wells's perfect day?

In the next day's newspapers, the Godwink emerged: David Wells and Don Larsen, the only perfect-game pitchers in Yankee history, had both attended Point Loma High School near San Diego and had both played for the school's baseball team—thirty-five years apart.

Fast-forward fourteen months to July 18, 1999. David Cone was in the final innings of what turned out to be another crowd-exploding perfect game. Here's the Larsen connection: on that day Don Larsen had been invited to fly in from Idaho to throw out the first pitch to his old catcher, Yogi Berra, for "Yogi Berra Day."

After David Cone's perfect game unfolded, Yankee fans showered their pitcher with uproarious accolades. But as the euphoric cacophony carried David Cone into the locker room, his most treasured praise came in a hug from Don Larsen—the only man connected to all three Yankee perfect games.

One more Godwink: Another player was integral to the second and third perfect games. Second baseman Chuck Knoblauch made the single most critical play to save both David Wells's game on May 17, 1998, and David Cone's on July 18, 1999. Wells had one out in the eighth when Minnesota Twin Ron Commer nailed a hard ground ball toward second base. It was a breath-catching moment. If the grounder got past Knoblauch, Wells's perfect game would have been blown. Knoblauch knocked it down, scooped it up, and threw to first for the out.

Then, in David Cone's perfect game, again with one out in the eighth inning came another hard grounder to Knoblauch. He dashed to the ball, fielded it backhanded, and threw to first for the out. In both cases, the hard grounders to Knoblauch came the closest to spoiling the perfect games.

When we're working hard to achieve our destiny, whether in sports, work, or relationships, sometimes it seems the winks come as if to help us celebrate our achievements and to affirm our efforts. This same type of affirmation, almost a pat on the back, was received by the player in the next story.

Perfect golf

A hole-in-one doesn't happen often in golf. Hitting the ball off the tee so perfectly that it flies all the way to the green and plunks into the hole in one single motion is the stuff of every golfer's dream.

In thirty-nine years of golf, Dave Wilson had never gotten one. And then, on the day it finally happened, it came with a wink. Upon arriving home triumphantly that day, Wilson found a birthday card, mailed four days earlier, from his son. What first caught his attention was the logo on the back of the card: a hole-in-one. His eyes widened as he took a look at the front of the card. A character was putting on the ninth green—the same hole on which he had gotten his hole-in-one earlier that day.

For Dave Wilson, the only thing more special about his hole-in-one was the Godwink that accompanied it.

Of all the seats . . .

Stories about sporting winks lead us to wonder if sometimes God isn't just having fun with us.

Take this one. Phil Regan felt like a fish out of water. The backyard barbecue was supposed to be a welcoming event for summer visitors to Martha's Vineyard off the coast of Cape Cod. Recognizing no one, Phil slipped through the back door of his host's home in search of a television for a quick look at the Boston Red Sox game. The television found, the party was quickly forgotten.

"How they doin'?"

Breaking Phil's solitude was the friendly voice of a man who confessed that he too was a dyed-in-the-wool Red Sox fan. In fact, he said, he wished he were at Fenway Park right then, using his season tickets.

Six weeks later, Phil and a friend decided to take the afternoon off and travel up to Boston to take in a Red Sox game. As was their practice, they bought two cheap "standing room only" tickets and waited several innings before surveying the stadium for better seats belonging to "no-shows."

Phil spotted two vacant seats beautifully located behind the Red Sox dugout, and he and his friend waited until the fourth inning before making their way down to them.

"Hey, these are great," remarked Phil, proud of himself for snaring such a prized vantage point.

His satisfaction didn't last long.

The tap on his shoulder came from a slightly familiar voice: "Do you know what seats you're supposed to be in?" The rightful owner was claiming his seats. Phil was flabbergasted. It was the same man who weeks earlier had engaged him in a friendly conversation about baseball at the barbecue. Out of 33,871 seats in Fenway Park, Phil and his friend had picked that man's seats.

The golfer and the missing child

Tim Simpson is a pro golfer of some note who plays on tour all around the country. To underscore his support for the National Center for Missing Children, Tim places a photo of a missing child on his golf bag during every tournament.

At the 1991 Masters Golf Tournament in Augusta, Georgia, Simpson had the computer-enhanced picture of Shannon Minor on his bag. The picture was only a computer simulation of what Shannon might look like as a nine-year-old. She had disappeared when she was only eighteen months old.

Five days later, the National Center for Missing Children received an anonymous telephone call from a woman. "Shannon Minor is in Houston," the caller said before hanging up.

After authorities brought Shannon back to her mother, there was speculation about whether someone had seen her picture on Simpson's golf bag. But the computer-enhanced picture of what an eighteen-month-old baby might look like at age nine didn't look much like Shannon. Further, no one who had watched the Master's Tournament on television could recall any close-ups of Tim Simpson's golf bag.

Simpson accepts the Godwink as divine alignment that someone—totally unrelated to and within five days of his placing Shannon's picture on the golf bag—happened to tip off authorities as to her whereabouts.

If you're a sports fan, you may have already recalled several sports-oriented Godwinks while reading the preceding stories.

When I told comedian Tim Conway the Don Larsen/New York Yankee story, he immediately responded by telling me a Godwink about baseball pitcher Bob Feller.

"Bob Feller's mother never saw him pitch, except for once," said Conway. "In that one game, she came to the ballpark—and was hit with a baseball."

Well, what should I have expected from a comedian?

Blessed is the one who perseveres under trial
because, having stood the test,
that person will receive the crown of life
that the Lord has promised to those who love him.

—JAMES 1:12 NIV

15

Career and Corporate Godwinks

We make a living by what we get.
We make a life by what we give.
Anonymous

As you journey to your destiny, you will occasionally find yourself at a crossroads in your career—a new path will suddenly appear, taking you into a whole new direction. It may be an unexpected opportunity that boosts your career. Or it may be a worrisome event such as a company takeover or a change in your employment status brought about by new people, new ideas, or new rules and regulations. Worse, it may be something that propels your livelihood to the very brink of disaster. Regardless of the circumstances, one thing is certain: you will feel *uncertain*.

And until your feelings of uncertainty can be converted to certainty, you will go through a period of discomfort. That's where Godwinks come into play. Winks from God are person-to-person messages of comfort just for you, to give you hope when you're surrounded by uncertainty.

As for companies themselves, it's enlightening to read about companies and corporations which have been influenced, directed, and sometimes saved by Godwinks. One little wink can change the entire course of a company's direction. Here are just a few:

The sticky accident

At 3M Company, the home of Scotch Tape, a research scientist named Dr. Spence Silver accidentally invented a new adhesive with odd qualities. It was made up of tiny spheres that were sticky individually, but because there was only intermittent contact, it would not stick strongly when coated onto tape backings. Silver knew it was a very unique adhesive, but he had no idea what to do with it.

Five years later, another 3M employee, Art Fry, was at church choir practice. He became frustrated when his scrap-paper bookmarks kept falling out of the choir hymnal. The falling bookmarks triggered a memory of a casual conversation with his colleague Dr. Silver, and sparked his idea to use Silver's adhesive for bookmarks.

Soon 3M had a new product line: Post-it Notes. One year after they were introduced in 1980, the small yellow pads were named the company's "Outstanding New Product." They've become an indispensable part of office life, thanks to the Godwink of a casual conversation between two 3M employees and falling bookmarks.

French fasteners

In 1941, a Frenchman named George de Mestral took his dog for a walk in the woods. Upon returning, he had the same problem most of us have encountered at one time or another after a walk outdoors: tiny burrs were stuck to his wool pants legs and to his dog's wagging tail.

But de Mestral did something most of us never have—he put his pants under a microscope to see *why* the burrs were sticking. He was fascinated to see the hundreds of little hooks in the burrs engaging the individual threads in the material of his pants.

Voila! Velcro was born. George de Mestral's walk in the woods provided the Godwink of insight leading to its invention.

The French words *vel*ours, meaning "hairy velvet," and *cro*chet, meaning "to hook," were neatly combined to create the Velcro name.

Look for the signs in your career

Innovations resulting from a flash of creative vision have altered the lifestyles of millions of people. Your life is also filled with these winks of insight which lead you down one path or another. These Godwinks can show you better ways to conduct your business, new ways to please your customers, or clever ways to save money.

As you read the following stories about people whose careers were guided by winks from God, keep your mind open to the possibilities that Godwinks can have on your own career.

Hugh Downs lands *20/20* job

In my new job overseeing ABC's *Good Morning America* television show, my mission was to catapult GMA past NBC's mighty *Today Show* in the ratings. I was only a few months into this job when GMA's host, David Hartman, was to go on vacation.

GMA's bookers recommended we use a Hollywood actor to replace him, but I wrestled with the merits of that notion, wondering how it would impact the show's credibility as a source for news. I pondered the question and then had a great idea: Why not try to get former *Today Show* host Hugh Downs, who was then nearly a decade into a quasi-retirement, to fill in for Hartman?

"Maybe we can win over some *Today Show* viewers," I reasoned with the bookers. When the week arrived for Hugh Downs to do his guest spot, everything proceeded according to plan. Although Downs quietly worried that perhaps network television had changed in the decade he had been away, he was the perfect image of confidence and authority each morning as the GMA theme began.

On Downs's second day, another big event was taking

place at the network. ABC News was launching a new prime-time magazine show called *20/20*. Unfortunately, the show's premier episode on a Tuesday evening garnered poor reviews for its hosts, both of whom had significant print journalism credentials and nearly none in television.

On Wednesday morning, ABC President Fred Pierce called an urgent meeting in his office with ABC News President Roone Arledge. He wanted to know what Arledge was going to do about the *20/20* flop.

As an embarrassed Arledge was about to uneasily answer that they were looking at other candidates for the host positions, the *Good Morning America* 10 A.M. West Coast feed came up on the closed-circuit television screen in Pierce's office, filling the room with a wonderfully authoritative voice: "I'm Hugh Downs. Good morning, America."

With a sudden, newfound confidence, Arledge, without skipping a beat, nodded to the screen and said, "I'm thinking about talking to *him*!" Of course he had not been thinking of Hugh Downs until that very moment when Hugh Downs was fortuitously, divinely aligned to be on that screen.

At week's end, Hugh Downs and I had lunch to celebrate his new job as host of *20/20*. It was a job he kept for the next twenty-one years.

Like Hugh Downs, there are times in your life when you think that you are traveling along the path you were meant to be on and suddenly something happens to take you off into a whole new direction. Keep yourself open to the possibility that the same kind of good fortune can happen to you.

And like Roone Arledge, keep your eyes open to the possibilities in front of you—both the planned ones and the surprise opportunities—so you don't miss the Godwinks that could make or break your career.

I hope these stories have shown you that your work is filled with Godwinks which can lead you down one path or another. And I hope that these examples of hope and encouragement will inspire you to watch for your Godwinks, then to marvel at the direct messages that you are receiving from above.

Acknowledging the existence of Godwinks seems to result in this phenomenon: You get more and more Godwinks!

The eyes of the Lord are in every place,
watching the evil and the good.

—PROVERBS 15:3 NASB

16

Little Serendipities

Be not afraid of life.
Believe that life is worth living,
and your belief will help create the fact.
William James

Most of the day-to-day Godwinks that happen to you are not big or life changing. Generally they're the small, sometimes whimsical little winks that make you quietly ask: Does that mean something?

Little winks *do* mean something: that you're never alone that God is constantly present in your life. Whenever I'm away from home, I am always fascinated by the number of street signs with the name Grant—which is also my son's name—that seem to pop up. I always conclude that I am receiving a little reminder, designed just for me, of the omnipresence of God's love that was so evident in my son's miraculous survival at birth.

More often than not, little Godwinks, like the big ones, are simply a message of hope and reassurance.

The day I interviewed Sybil Puruczky for the job as my executive assistant, she said she had two daughters.

"What are their names?" I inquired.

"Morgan and Taylor."

"No kidding," I smiled. "I have one niece and one granddaughter. One named Morgan, the other named Taylor."

That wink was confirmation that I was on the right track. It was the beginning of a long, wonderful working relationship with Sybil, one of the best executive assistants I have ever had.

By the way, there was one other coincidence: *my* Morgan and Taylor share the same birthday, May 23—and it turned out that Sybil began working for me during the week of May 23.

Godwinky humor

Those who post comments and stories on the Godwink Facebook page have frequently said that "Godwinks are God's way of showing His sense of humor." I've subscribed to that every time I've come across someone whose name matched their occupation. For instance,

- The Woods Hole Oceanographic Institute in Massachusetts is where marine biologist Evelyn Fish once worked.

- At All Souls Church in New York City the pastor was Dr. Forrest Church.
- A Long Island, New York, dentist was named Dr. E. Z. Fillum.
- On Fifth Avenue in New York City is where you could find the office of dermatologist Dr. Jonathan Zizmor.
- In Washington, D.C., a radio traffic reporter was named Mary Driver.
- In Gulfport, Mississippi, a physical fitness trainer was named Constant Payne.
- In Tulsa, Oklahoma, there was a physician named Dr. Safety R. First.
- Jack Frost issued forecasts at the Weather Bureau in Oregon.

Your winks from God can be something of a riddle, something ironic, or just something triggering a smile and a shake of your head. But when they happen, *you* know—it's a special message just for you.

The winks of someone on your mind

How often has someone crossed your mind that you hadn't thought of for years, and then the phone rings and it's that person? Or perhaps someone was on your mind, and a wink from God seemed to say, "Yep. You should have been thinking of them."

One Sunday in church, our preacher told of a project he'd been involved with called "silent prayer partners." The idea was to pray for someone without their knowing that you were praying for them.

"What a great idea," I thought, looking around the church. I spotted a couple sitting three pews ahead of me—Belle and Bruce Reynolds. "I'll pray for them all week long without their knowing about it," I decided. And every evening for the next week, my son, Grant, and I included "God bless Belle and Bruce" in our evening prayers.

The following Sunday morning, I arrived at church a bit late. Slipping into my pew, I noted that the ushers were completing a passing-of-the-baskets, which struck me as odd. It is the custom of my church to take no offering. Instead, offertory boxes are at the rear.

At coffee hour, one of the ushers, Forbes Linkhorn, walked up to me carrying a basket. Inside were three little scraps of folded paper. "SQuire," he exclaimed, thrusting the basket toward me, "You didn't get your silent prayer partner."

I looked at him, puzzled.

"We decided to take the idea Ted mentioned last week and start our own silent prayer partners. We put the names of the congregation in a basket, and everyone picked out someone to pray for this week," he continued.

I remained hesitant as Forbes again pushed the basket

toward me. "But," I whined, "I already *have* prayer partners—*two* of them—Belle and Bruce Reynolds."

He smiled, still extending the basket.

"Oh, well," I mumbled, "I guess we can have more than one or two prayer partners." I pulled out one of the three slips of paper left in the basket, unfolded it, and read the contents. My mouth must have dropped.

Out of 600 church members whose names could have been on those scraps of paper, here's what mine said: "Belle and Bruce Reynolds."

Aren't these the times in life when you just glance heavenward and say, "OK, God, the joke's on me!" At those times, it seems like God isn't just winking, but He also has a smile on His face and might be slapping His knee.

The winks of finding things

What about those times when you are looking and looking for something and—in the blink of a wink—it serendipitously appears?

Prominent historian Thomas Fleming told me about the time he was frustrated with his difficulty in finding information about the legendary World War II hero Eddie Rickenbacher—particularly his survival at sea on a raft. As Fleming combed the backroom stacks at the New York Public Library, he was about to give up when his hand plucked from the shelf a thin book covered with dust. It was written by a man he had never heard of, the pilot of a plane that had crashed at sea during the war. The pilot/author had been picked up and rescued by another crash survivor on a raft—Eddie Rickenbacher.

The whole story that Fleming was looking for was right there.

Godwinks with numbers

One also thinks about God's sense of humor when numbers seem to defy the laws of chance. My friend Gordon Hyatt told me that the numerals 5 and 4 keep reappearing in his life.

"I grew up at 45 Westmoreland Avenue, and the family friends with whom we always spent Thanksgiving lived at 54 Hopkins Place," he said. "Fifty-four miles away, my father bought a store at 54 Main Street."

In 1954, Hyatt experienced a turning point in his education, significantly altering his course into the field of dramatic arts. That led him into television at CBS as a news and documentary producer at the network's Westside studios, where the street number is 245.

Godwinks with dates

Sometimes there are serendipitous numerical Godwinks relating to dates. Nobel Prize–winning physicist Stephen

Hawking's book *A Brief History of Time* discusses such things as the Big Bang theory of the birth of the universe and the meaning of black holes in space.

Hawking was born January 8, 1942, the three-hundredth anniversary of the death of Galileo, who is called the world's first physicist and the first person to use a telescope in exploring the universe.

Yield to the signs

Along every highway are big signs and little signs. They all have meaning. You wouldn't accept or dismiss a road sign because of its size, would you?

I hope you will also never dismiss *your* little signs, your winks from God, which are being placed along your path for a reason—even if that reason is no more than a gentle jab in the shoulder, a pat on the back, or a dose of humor to lift your spirits.

Like a wink from your grandfather, these winks are communicating God's message to you: "Hey kid, I'm thinking about you—right now."

> *There is a time for everything,*
> *and a season for every activity under the heaven.*
> —ECCLESIASTES 3 NIV

Conclusion

By and by, God caught his eye.
McCord

The definition of "coincidence" found in the *American Heritage Dictionary* is "A sequence of events that although accidental seems to have been planned or arranged." This definition, of course, begs the question, "Planned or arranged by whom?"

Most people will answer, "By God, that's who." God is not just an architect of the past but of the very minute-by-minute designer, navigator, and weaver of our present lives.

So if our life has an architect, what's our role in it?

Well, it's not just to sit on the sidelines watching our life unfold. We can affect our future and our destiny, by accepting that Godwinks are there to lift our spirits and to see that our choices are right. The Godwinks we receive are His pats on the back to keep us going, keep us hopeful, and keep us fully alive.

We just need to accept that while life is often a mystery, each of us has a role in helping the mystery unfold.

We need to acknowledge that God is communicating to each of us—every day—through Godwink messages just for us.

So from now on, whenever a Godwink pops up at a particularly auspicious moment in your life, I hope you will come to say, "I-e-e-e wonder. Was that a Godwink?"

Chances are pretty good that it was.